CONSTELLATIONS

T0313461

Like the future itself, the imaginative possibilities of science fiction are limitless. And the very development of cinema is inextricably linked to the genre, which, from the earliest depictions of space travel and the robots of silent cinema to the immersive 3D wonders of contemporary blockbusters, has continually pushed at the boundaries. **Constellations** provides a unique opportunity for writers to share their passion for science fiction cinema in a book-length format, each title devoted to a significant film from the genre. Writers place their chosen film in a variety of contexts – generic, institutional, social, historical – enabling **Constellations** to map the terrain of science fiction cinema from the past to the present... and the future.

'This stunning, sharp series of books fills a real need for authoritative, compact studies of key science fiction films. Written in a direct and accessible style by some of the top critics in the field, brilliantly designed, lavishly illustrated and set in a very modern typeface that really shows off the text to best advantage, the volumes in the **Constellations** series promise to set the standard for SF film studies in the 21st century.'
Wheeler Winston Dixon, Ryan Professor of Film Studies, University of Nebraska

 Constellations

 Constelbooks

Also available in this series

Close Encounters of the Third Kind Jon Towlson

Inception David Carter

Forthcoming

Altered States John Edmond

Robocop Omar Ahmed

Seconds Jez Conolly

These are the Damned Nick Riddle

CONSTELLATIONS

BLADE RUNNER

Sean Redmond

Sean Redmond

is Associate Professor of Media and Communication at Deakin University, Australia. He has research interests in East Asian cinema, film authorship, genre, whiteness and stardom and celebrity. His numerous books include *Endangering Science Fiction Film* (AFI Film Readers), *A Companion to Celebrity* (as co-editor) and *Studying Chungking Express*.

Acknowledgements

Thanks to Stu, Deborah and Karen for kind advice and some excellent proofreading support. And thanks also to John for his patience.

Dedication

For Charlie, wherever-you-are.

First published in 2008 as *Studying Blade Runner*. This revised edition published 2016 by Auteur, 24 Hartwell Crescent, Leighton Buzzard LU7 1NP
www.auteur.co.uk
Copyright © Auteur 2016

Series design: Nikki Hamlett at Cassels Design
Set by Cassels Design www.casselsdesign.co.uk
Printed and bound by CPI Group (UK) Ltd, Croydon, CR0 4YY

Cover image © Warner Bros./BFI Stills
All stills © Warner Bros./Movie Market except pages 27, 41, 50, 62 and 77 © Warner Bros./Joel Finler Archive; page 43 © BFI Stills; and pages 71-76, 79 and 88, taken from the Region 2 DVD.

British Library Cataloguing-in-Publication Data
A catalogue record for this book is available from the British Library

ISBN paperback: 978-1-911325-09-3
ISBN ebook: 978-1-911325-10-9

Contents

UK poster for the original theatrical release, 1982

Introduction: Reading (into) the Greatest Science Fiction Film Ever Made

Harrison Ford as Deckard

> Few things reveal so sharply as science fiction the wishes, hopes, fears, inner stresses and tensions of an era, or define its limitations with such exactness. (H.L. Gold in Kuhn, 1990)

Blade Runner (1982, Director's Cut, 1992, Final Cut, 2007) has become one of the most lauded science fiction films ever made. Cult fans dedicate websites to it, such as *The Replicant Site*, and organise conventions to consider again and again its cultural and aesthetic merits, and to offer collective answers and solutions to its ambiguous or open-ended narrative. Academics have written about it in terms of its racial and sexual politics, its exploration of humanity, and of the way it challenges many of the accepted/expected codes and conventions of the science fiction film. *Blade Runner* is considered by the British Film Institute to be a 'Modern Classic' (see Scott Bukatman's excellent book, 1997), and is often one of the most written about films when it comes to science fiction readers such as Annette Kuhn's *Alien Zone* (1990). Science fiction courses, such as the one I run at Victoria University of Wellington, use *Blade Runner* as the seminal text with which to explore the poetics and politics of the science fiction genre more widely. *Blade Runner* gets repeat viewing on late night terrestrial television, and its visual and narrative influence extends not only to other science fiction films, such as *Dark City* (1998) and *Natural City* (2003), but to fictional films more generally, such as the rain-soaked thriller, *Se7en* (1995). *Blade Runner*, with its dystopian future, nihilistic impulses, psychopathic cyborgs and mesmerising cityscapes is a film that seems to effect profoundly those who come into contact with it – so much so that one can argue that it acts as a doorway into the wishes, hopes, fears, inner stresses and tensions of an era that now stretches beyond the 25 years or so since the film's making.

This, of course, was not always the case. The film's opening weekend receipts were disappointingly just over $6 million, and by the time Warner Bros. decided to pull the film from distribution, due to these poor and declining ticket sales, *Blade Runner* had made only $14.5 million at the box-office, making it one of the biggest commercial failures of the summer, bringing in less than half the cost of its production. Critics struggled with the film also: Variety (16 June 1982) called it 'dramatically muddled', while Gene Siskel of the Chicago Tribune argued that the film 'looks terrific but is empty at its core' (25 June 1982). The initial commercial and critical reception for *Blade Runner* was little short of disastrous.

However, if one were to examine the history of cinema, or in fact the history of almost any art form, one would find countless examples of a film being poorly received, or an artist's piece of work being lambasted, only to eventually become accepted as a masterpiece of its genre/form. Alfred Hitchcock's Vertigo (1958) is one such film example, while the misunderstood genius of the painter Van Gough another. In fact, films that innovate, trouble or straddle the commercial with the artistic (as *Blade Runner* surely does) often suffer from this sort of misunderstanding and critical mauling. One might contentiously argue that one of the acid tests for whether a film is truly great or not is whether it was misunderstood or poorly received on its initial release.

Blade Runner dared to be generically and culturally different. Against the rise of the science fiction blockbuster in the late 1970s and the repeated promise of action, special effects and awesome spectacle by films such as *Star Wars* (1977), *Blade Runner* instead 'layered' its depressing, noirish *mise-en-scène* and laboured over its intricate storytelling. *Blade Runner* meditated on the nature of human existence, explored humanity and talked seriously about the (post)modern world, while other science fiction films of the time took you on a cinematic roller-coaster ride that left you breathless but ultimately disappointed.

Commercial science fiction films of the period generally offered up utopian solutions to earth-bound crises, often in the form of an Alien Messiah figure who comes to represent hope and redemption to faulty, failing human lives. In *E.T.* (1982) the loveable, cuddly, healing hands of E.T. rescue Eliott's one parent family from disintegration so that by the end of the film each family member has come to know their true worth through E.T. In *Blade Runner*, by contrast, narrative ambiguity and a partly inexplicable sense of loss and alienation permeate the entire film, and by narrative closure the only thing certain is that certainty itself (over one's identity and how long one can or will live) has disappeared beneath the skin of humans who could well be robots, and robots who could well be humans. *Blade Runner*, for all its concealed and revealed humanity, examined the modern world through a dark lens. This is a virtual 'doorway' worth entering, then, if only to discover more about ourselves and the world we really live in.

There are a total of seven different versions of *Blade Runner* that have been screened to date: the workprint (1982); the San Diego sneak preview (1982); the US Theatrical Release (1982); the International Theatrical Release (1982, the version shown in the UK); the U.S. Broadcast version (1986); the Director's Cut (1992); and the Final Cut (2007). However, for the purpose of this guide two versions of the film will be analysed: the original US theatrical release of 1982 (only marginally different from the International release) and the Director's Cut of 1992.

Because of poor test screenings where people complained about a confusing plot and a dour ending, the original theatrically released version has a studio enforced voice-over narration (delivered by Rick Deckard/Harrison Ford), and a 'romantic' ending that shows Deckard and Rachael (Sean Young) escaping from the city into an idyllic mountain landscape (footage that was actually taken from the out-takes of Stanley Kubrick's horror film, *The Shining* (1980)). This utopian ending in part suggests some sort of narrative closure. The voice-over is removed in the Director's Cut and the ending, now set in the city, perhaps symbolically suggests that Deckard is a replicant, whose own death is therefore imminent and whose entire life has been built on a photographic lie.

In this study of *Blade Runner* explicit reference will only be made to the two different cuts when the similarities and differences between them throw up interesting issues and arguments – as will be the case, for example, when addressing the constraints put on directors in the production process.

Studying *Blade Runner* is divided into five areas of investigation, areas that mirror the five key concepts of much media analysis: Genre, Narrative, Representation, Institutions (Authors) and Audiences. Much of the work will involve close textual analysis of the film but this will be supported by reference to wider cultural and ideological issues, and to production and reception contexts. What I hope to do is get beneath the surface of the film to reveal its hidden messages and textual complexities. This is a work of textual excavation and contextual appreciation. It is a study very much in keeping, then, with the rational, clinical and yet ultimately humanist methods that are employed by Deckard himself to hunt down the replicants in *Blade Runner*.

Since I can remember I have been in love with science fiction film and television. The light saber was always my toy of choice, the science fiction season the only thing worth staying in or up for on TV. I would stand in the garden and stare at the stars, imagining time travel and alien encounters. I still do. When I first watched *Blade Runner*, on late night TV in the early 1980s, I was so moved by the film that I spoke about its architecture and existential angst (if not in those words!) for weeks – to my Mum and Dad, sisters, school friends, relatives, even to people whom I normally wouldn't speak to. This study guide evolves out of this love, a labour of love, and I hope that if you are not already in love with the film you very soon will be.

Synopsis

Los Angeles, 2019. Five NEXUS 6 Androids or 'Replicants' have rebelled against their 'maker', Dr. Tyrell and the Tyrell Corporation. They have arrived on Earth from 'Off-World' to discover when they were 'born' so that they can in turn know when their pre-programmed deaths will be. They also seek revenge on those humans who designed them to have such a limited life-span in the first place. Ex-Blade Runner (a particular variety of law-enforcer), Rick Deckard, is forced out of retirement to handle the assignment to kill – or 'retire' – them. In the course of his investigations Deckard falls in love with Rachael, one of Dr. Tyrell's most advanced replicants. It is in part through discovering the truth about her replicant status that Deckard finally comes to question his own human identity. An archetypal anti-hero, Deckard kills three of the rebels and fights a final battle with the lead replicant, Roy Batty, in the derelict, rain-soaked Bradbury building. Roy Batty emerges triumphant but instead of allowing Deckard to fall to his death, rescues him, moments before his own programmed life-span comes to an end. In the original 1982 release, Gaff, a fellow policeman, allows Deckard and Rachael to escape to the country away from the suffocating city. In the 'Director's Cut', and subsequent 'Final Cut', the film ends in the city, with an uncertain future for Deckard (and Rachael) since by the film's closure he has arguably also been revealed to be a replicant.

I. Genre

Genre analysis came relatively late to Film Studies. As Annette Kuhn (1990) observes,

> Its origins (usually dated to the late 1950s) lay in a populist reaction to the perceived elitism of a film criticism which stressed authorship – the genius or the creativity of one individual, usually male, and usually the director – as the key to understanding films.

Genre analysis, by contrast, attended to the shared visual and narrative codes and conventions that could be detected across a body of filmwork, regardless of who was making the film. So, for example, the western could be examined through its generically specific iconography of stetsons, six-guns, horses, cattle plains, wagon trains, ranches, cowboys, saloon girls, etc. and its narrativised binary oppositions – garden : wilderness, insider : outsider, individual : community.

However, the move to genre-based analysis was also predicated upon the recognition that the Hollywood cinema machine pre-sold and packaged films according to genre related impulses. Posters, press packs, adverts and merchandising all spoke in the signs and codes of genre, and films were green-lit on the basis of their likely generic appeal. Today, one only has to think about how films such as *The Matrix* (1999) and *I, Robot* (2004) are marketed to see how central the genre of science fiction is to films' promotional imagery and sound bites.

Appeal, and pleasure and subject positioning were also given serious consideration under the umbrella of genre analysis: spectators were increasingly placed centre stage and their engagement with these supposedly repetitive commercial forms critically examined. For the first time in Film Studies popular art or mass entertainment was being examined on its own merits. Genre analysis gave critical weight to film texts that had been previously labelled as 'low art' or commercial nonsense, and to audiences who had been viewed as passive dupes.

Genre analysis, nonetheless, immediately ran into a number of problems; the first being what might be referred to as an 'empiricist dilemma' (Kuhn, 1990). When one attempted to find the origins of a film genre, to go to the very first example of, say, a western, one was faced with the issue of having to use established codes and conventions that had supposedly only emerged after a period of time – after the very first western had been made in fact. This dilemma posed the unanswerable question: how can a 'western' exist *before* its specific visual and narrative codes and conventions have been isolated and established?

Another problem with genre analysis was classification and transformation. When one began to try to put together criteria for what constituted the codes and conventions of a particular genre one found slippage and leakage in terms of consistency in *mise-en-scène* and what were supposedly established narrative patterns. This was because while genre was/is always about repetition and prediction it is also about innovation and renewal. Genre films often try to offer something new and something unexpected in their visual language or storytelling modes. This notion of subtle transformation is tied to both production changes, such as more money being directed to genres that are successful commercially, audience demands, and wider historical and cultural transformations. If one were to examine, for example, the B-movie science fiction films of the 1950s with their 1990 counterparts one would, in the main, discover a world of difference in terms of imagery, special effects and narrative concerns. The fear of the Cold War between the USA and Russia dominated the cardboard cut-out look and feel of 1950s sci-fi; while the terrors and pleasures of cyberspace and genetic engineering dominate the concerns of the lavishly produced contemporary sci-fi film.

Hybridity was also a related problem when trying to pin down the specifics of a film genre. Films such as *Calamity Jane* (1953) could be identified as a western, but also as a musical, comedy and romance. Many films, in fact, can be 'unpacked' in this way, not least *Star Wars* which one contemporary critic argued is a western set in space! Of course, the notion of hybridity neatly leads into *Blade Runner*, a film that combines the codes of science fiction with film noir and the police story. But first, an introduction to science fiction more generally.

What is Genre? What is Science Fiction?

Over the last 25 years or so the science fiction film has come to dominate the production and distribution landscape of Hollywood. Each summer, a new, more expensive, more spectacularly lavish sci-fi film makes it to our cinemas to thrill and entertain us. Special effects, once the 'home' of science fiction, stitch together films from all genres, making the 'awe and wonder' factor of science fiction commonplace. Some of the top grossing films of all time are science fiction films – including *E.T.*, *Jurassic Park* (1997), *Avatar* (2009) and, of course, the most recent entry into the *Star Wars* universe, *The Force Awakens* (2015). Science fiction, in short, is one of the most important film genres being produced in contemporary Hollywood.

Science fiction can be defined through its recurring *narrative themes*, its shared *visual iconographies*, and its *mode of address* or particular storytelling apparatus – audiences are addressed in highly specific ways in the science fiction film. I want to now briefly examine these in turn.

Annette Kuhn argues, in relation to genre study generally, 'Perhaps more interesting, and probably more important, than what a film genre *is* is the question of what, in cultural terms, it does – its "cultural instrumentality"'(1990). Cultural instrumentality refers to the way that genre films have an interdependent relationship with the real world at the time they are made. Genre films, all-be-it subtextually or allegorically, deal with the fears, hopes, panics and anxieties that circulate in wider society, bringing these issues or *themes* into the belly of the film under the disguise of a western, gangster or science fiction scenario. Genre films, then, interpret what is going on in the real world and contribute to the way the real world is understood through devices which divert one's attention away from considering it to be 'real' or to be about one's real life.

In terms of science fiction, a whole series of cultural fears are played out through the overall distancing device that *alternative possibilities* are being entertained in the text. These possibilities allow for alternative futures, social structures, human relationships, lifestyles and technologies to be imagined, but imagined in a way that through code and symbol simultaneously speak to the present – to the here and now. Science fiction does this looking to the future but speaking about the present in two different and often opposing ways.

First, science fiction's alternative possibilities are conjured up through the disaster/ dystopian narrative. In this scenario, the future is one of apocalypse and despair. The world has been taken over by cyborgs, clones or automatons, or technology/ techno-science has more widely produced a society where human emotion has been extinguished or is on the run from these hyper-rationalist/scientific forces (see *The Matrix* or *Terminator* series). Alternatively, consumerism, globalisation, corporate greed and media dumbing down and disinformation have so taken a hold on the power bases of the world, and the ordering of everyday life, that freedoms have been eroded and life is given meaning only in relation to the amount of dollars it can accrue or the amount of TV time it garners. The poor, the weak, the racially Other are often forcibly excluded from these future worlds. Natural resources are scarce and the synthetic, the manufactured and the virtual dominate everything from eating habits to sleeping arrangements. Privacy has been outlawed and the only family one belongs to is the corporate state, or the one found online. In *The Running Man* (1987), television airs and organises murder trials like a game show and the Presidency has its own entertainment division. The masses are kept diverted and under control through the propaganda of the visual image, which is everywhere, and personal freedoms are kept in check by totalitarian police and army regimes that kill 'rebels' on sight.

In a post 9/11 context, science fiction film has become increasingly concerned with war-centred invasion narratives. These invasion texts arguably speak to the range of fears that circulate in a catastrophic climate of insecurity brought about by 'The War on Terror' and its corollary, 'The War on the West'. As Derek Kompare argues, in relation to three first season 2005 USA television invasion texts – *Invasion* (Shaun Cassidy, ABC), *Threshold* (Bragi F. Schut, CBS), and *Surface* (Jonas Pate, NBC) – 'the core of insecurity is the idea that nowhere is absolutely safe, that nobody is absolutely trustworthy... the alien menaces... are practically invisible... the outside threat could come from within' (2005).

For example, Steven Spielberg's re-make of *War of the Worlds* (2005) is full of the imagery and symbolism of 9/11 catastrophe; and of a number of the leitmotifs of the War on Terror. Ray Ferrier (Tom Cruise) is a blue-collar worker from New Jersey, estranged from his family, who during the course of the film proves his worth as a father/heroic male. If not quite the mythic fire fighter of 9/11, Ferrier nonetheless crawls through the rubble, the twisted metal and the burning fires to keep his children/child alive. The film is shot through with 9/11 war imagery: burning planes fall out of the sky; military missiles slice through the air; the alien enemy, intent on harvesting all of humankind for their own survival and domination, emerge fully armoured from *within* the borders of New York City. Human blood, in the literal sense, soaks the screen – the entire *mise-en-scène* – as if the social body of America, where the film is entirely contained, is being bled to death. The defeat of the aliens emerges in two, perhaps contradictory ways. Ferrier's transformation into a warrior-male enables him to repel repeated attacks and to take his child 'home'. Pivotally, he learns how to kill and kill 'American', in the most 'intimate' or proximate of ways, when he silences (strangles) the deranged Harlan Ogilvy (Tim Robbins) because he threatens to give their position away. His heroic actions refuse to let America be over-taken, over-run, and he will protect America from wayward Americans. Ferris (Cruise) stands, then, as a symbol of America's resilience and hyper-masculine strength when it is tested most.

However, the aliens are in the end vanquished not by heroic act, guile, invention or techno-militaristic co-operation (as is often the case in science fiction cinema), but by a common air-borne virus. At the end of the film, alien space ships crash to the ground and their bodies fall from their interiors, emaciated, because the very air is poisonous to them. The aliens that first emerged from beneath/within America – as co-coordinated 'terrorist' cells – are beaten by a home-grown virus that is itself terrorist-like – invisible and yet everywhere. The barely-hidden premise of the film, then, is that America can no longer rely on conventional warfare to kill the enemy (that lies within), it has to adapt, mutate; it has to become (like) the enemy in order to survive.

Second, science fiction's future worlds are imagined in terms of the utopian narrative or the structuring theme that the future is bright, harmonious and in many cases miraculous. In these utopian visions, technology has allowed humankind to travel across time and space, and techno-science has cured cancers, infertility, and in some cases can cheat death. In these new world orders, once warring nation states have unified and tackled new problems off-world. Poverty has been eradicated and liberal democracy ensures that prejudice and nepotism no longer take place. The *Star Trek* franchise best exemplifies this utopian vision with its multi-racial/national crew, its life-healing technologies and its liberal democratic political structure.

Unlike other film genres, such as the western or the gangster film, science fiction has a much more loosely defined set of visual codes or iconographies. This is in part because science fiction can be set in the past, present or future and the worlds that are visited there can be stripped bare of invention and difference so that they look just like the world we presently live in or did once. It is also because the possibilities for the visual landscape of science fiction are that much more extensive since science fiction is so often *about* visual invention. Nonetheless, there are a number of shared iconographies that would put one in a conventional science fiction film.

New weaponry, clothing, transportation, architecture and sentient species are often the central key markers for entry into a science fiction world. Lasers, light sabers, phasers, etc., suggest a world of evolved precision-crafted weaponry. Silver suits, space suits, oxygen masks, space helmets, crystal uniforms, etc., help visualise the futuristic nature of sci-fi but also the power relationships between people. Flying cars, spacecraft, hoverboards, time machines and teleporters so increase movement that time and space become conflated, disconnected, increasingly crowded and totally universal. One is seen simply flying through time and across different planes and realms of space in the science fiction film. Vast edifices of aluminium and steel, bubbles made of polystyrene, and whole cities that rise seemingly into infinity provide the futuristic setting, subverting perspective, increasing social division in their high : low organisation, and re-imagining, at the same time, the concept of home and work. Aliens, Alien Messiahs and extra-terrestrials populate the narratives of science fiction, sometimes bringing terror, sometimes celestial-like hope, but always in a visually striking form – with tentacles, bug-eyes, wide-eyes, phallic and razor sharp teeth, etc.

However, and in sum, science fiction best visualises itself through the articulation or relationship *between* these iconographies. Proton phasers that fire from warp speed space ships at alien marauders as a worm hole approaches, firmly place one, at least visually, in a science fiction text.

Science fiction has a particular mode of address or way of engaging with and involving audiences in their possible alternative realities. This has been best expressed by Annette Kuhn as 'complete sensory and bodily engulfment' (1999). Science fiction addresses or bombards all the human senses through its kinetic, highly charged and yet sensuous and cerebral stimulus. On the one hand science fiction is all about making the audience giddy with its hyper-fluid and breathtaking creations; on the other it asks the audience to ponder over these creations, to feel and think through them as more than just special effect since they often attempt to say something profound about the human condition. In one sense, according to Barry Keith Grant (1999) science fiction addresses the spectator as a 'wide-eyed child' – as one who is caught in a state of awe and wonder as the shots of deep space, new horizons, galactic travel and cityscapes dramatically appear on the retina of the frame/lens.

In the *Star Trek* film and television franchise, the Enterprise is repeatedly shot streaking, glowing, humming across the starlit sky, technically and scientifically magnificent. It is also shot from beneath, in a stationary position, to place the spectator as accomplice ethnographer on the voyages that are about to be undertaken. Kent A. Ono argues in relation to *Star Trek: The Next Generation* (1987-1994):

> ...the spectator's perspective below the ship emphasises the awesome power of both military and communications technology. The Enterprise hails the spectator to pay close attention to the opening sequence that foregrounds the entire episode and also cues the viewer to her own privileged viewing position, perhaps in her own spaceship from which to observe impending events – an ethnographic perch from which to document "native life". (Ono, 1996: 162)

Of course, one of the central ways that science fiction addresses the audience is through the spectacle of special effects or the partly self-conscious display of technological wizardry. In science fiction, while the 'how' of special effects is meant to be effaced or made invisible within the diegesis of the film, the knowledge that one is watching a state of the art effects sequence is meant to manifest in the 'wow! that's incredible!' moment that accompanies these scenes. So in one sense the pleasure of science fiction is a pleasure of the special effect.

Blade Runner as Science Fiction

In terms of its themes, iconographies and mode of address it seems pretty clear why *Blade Runner* falls within the science fiction genre. In fact so dystopian, iconic and visually spectacular is the film that it can be argued to be an exemplary case study for what constitutes a science fiction film.

Thematically, the film offers us a despairing view of the future. This is immediately represented through the crowded and media-saturated city space that is Los Angeles 2019. The film constantly returns us to high, low and expansive shots of the Gothic/ patch-work city as it belches flames, chokes on its own smog, and produces the discernible sense of an omnipresent decay that eats into the very fabric of the (street level) buildings. As Giuliana Bruno (1990) observes,

> The city of *Blade Runner* is not the ultramodern, but the postmodern city. It is not an orderly layout of skyscrapers and ultracomfortable, hypermechanized interiors. Rather, it creates an aesthetic of decay, exposing the dark side of technology, the process of disintegration.

Blade Runner is all about disintegration: earth is so over-populated and polluted that (white) people are encouraged, through adverts that adorn everything from mobile advertising hoardings to the sides of hi-rise buildings, to move to off-world colonies. Advertising, consumer goods, media and consumer conglomerates fuel the economy and indoctrinate the populace. Anything can be bought and sold on the black market because the city itself has become one giant marketplace – a metaphoric Chinatown no less. The city is chaotic, crisis driven: made up at the lower levels of waste, acid rain, tumble down dwellings, hovels, faceless racial Others, and a maze of dangerous side-streets. Deckard eats here, confronts and kills two of the replicants here, but retires to his apartment in the higher levels to escape the filth and the squalor that he is nonetheless attracted to. According to Ridley Scott, (quoted in Sammon, 1999):

> One of the major visual ideas we had for BR was 'retrofitting', this overlaying of pre-existing architecture with patch jobs that side-steps the problem of tearing down old structures and replacing them with new ones.

This 'aesthetic of decay' is compounded by the open display of technology and the encroachment of technology and techno-science into all areas of social life so that the very nature of what the 'real' is, and what it means to be human, becomes blurred in the film. In *Blade Runner*, simulation and the synthetic reach into all areas of social life. Surveillance and media devices are everywhere – in fact one only really knows that one is human through an electronic emotional response test. The geneticist J.F. Sebastian surrounds himself with cyberpets and suffers from 'accelerated decrepitude', a wasting away disease that ages him prematurely – as if he is himself a genetic experiment gone wrong. The towering Tyrell Corporation building is a mock Egyptian edifice that overlooks the *image* of the Egyptian pyramids. Deckard is possibly revealed to be a replicant (expressed more explicitly in the Director's Cut), living an artificial lie about the nature of his own origin.

Blade Runner, then, taps into real concerns about techno-science, globalisation, population flows, media manipulation and environmental catastrophe that were in circulation at the time of the film's release and are, if anything, more prevalent today. The 1980s were a time of media corporate takeovers that saw the rise, for example, of the Murdoch media empire. The first stories about the hole in the ozone layer appeared, and recurrent fears about genetic engineering found their way into the press. Asia was imagined to be an economic and cultural threat to the hegemony of the west with the emergence of Sony and Honda as super-companies. Migration and immigration were seen as threats to national identity (in Britain, the then Prime Minister, Margaret Thatcher, referred to immigration as a 'swamping' problem). Michael Ryan and Douglas Kellner (1990) locate a specific critique of modern capitalism in the film, suggesting that,

> *Blade Runner* calls attention to the oppressive core of capitalism and advocates revolt against exploitation. The Tyrell Corporation invents replicants in order to have a more pliable labour force, and the film depicts how capitalism turns humans into machines.

In terms of iconography *Blade Runner* has many of the visual trademarks of the science fiction film. Flying cars called 'spinners' move menacingly across the landscape. 'Trafficators' direct the flow of traffic and people. Advertising 'blimps'

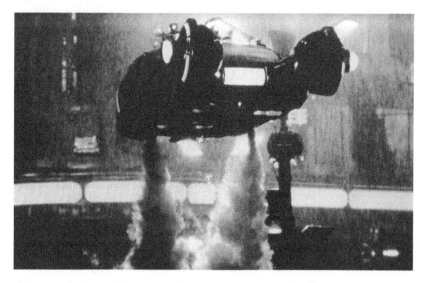

Blade Runner's *'spinner' flying car – a classic visual trademark of sci-fi-film*

hover above the city promoting a 'better life' 'Off-world'. The entire cityscape is nightmarishly futuristic: it constantly pours with acid rain and the sun is partly blotted out because of the pollution. There is no discernible difference between night and day in *Blade Runner*. People have neon reflectors in their umbrellas to get around. The media are an omnipresent force – one cannot go anywhere in Los Angeles 2019 without media technology shaping one's behaviour. In short, in one clear sense the entire *mise-en-scène* of *Blade Runner* speaks the visual language of dystopian science fiction.

But on a sonic level too, the futuristic synth score, by Vangelis, anchors the technophobic visual field of the film. The haunting electronic pulse of the soundtrack adds semiotic weight to the dystopian images and settings that hold the film together. At key moments in fact the music almost seems to weep in (to) the film. And as Ridley Scott comments, 'every incident, every sound, every movement, every colour, every set, prop or actor has significance within the performance of the film' (quoted in Bukatman, 1997).

Nonetheless, it is *Blade Runner*'s mode of address that also positions the audience within a science fiction film. From the opening panoramic long shot of a brooding futuristic LA, the audience is treated to a visual extravaganza in which spectacle and display dominate the screen and stimulate the pleasures on offer. *Blade Runner* functions in terms of awe and wonder but this is also tinged with melancholy and introspection since *Blade Runner* City is a paradoxical ugly/beautiful place. One is asked to marvel at the textures in the spaces of the city while recoiling at what these spaces have come to mean. In fact, the ugly/beautiful introspection of *Blade Runner* is one of the things that makes its genre classification more difficult or rather more complex to identify, as I will now go onto suggest.

Blade Runner as Film Noir

Blade Runner is also clearly marked by some of the key visual and narrative motifs of film noir, a downbeat, investigative genre that emerged in the 1940s. In fact, Ridley Scott has described the overall design of *Blade Runner* as 'set forty years hence, made in the style of forty years ago' (Bukatman, 1997).

Deckard, the world weary and alienated ex-cop, is reminiscent of the Humphrey Bogart, Private Eye character, found in such films such as *The Maltese Falcon* (1941). Rachael is the archetypal 1940s *femme fatale*: mysterious, sexually dangerous and potentially duplicitous. (Critics such as Bukatman have noted how much she resembles the wronged Mildred Pierce from *Mildred Pierce* (1945), or the double-crossing character Phyllis Dietrichson from *Double Indemnity* (1944).) The down-beat voice-over narration of the original release, allowing Deckard to recall events that have already happened, is a device also borrowed from film noir and one that closes down the options for a happy ending (since the protagonist is always caught looking back mournfully). The moral ambiguity found in all the central characters is again a feature of film noir: trust, morality, and the lines between good and evil, right and wrong are blurred in *Blade Runner* as they are in films such as *Touch of Evil* (1958). Deckard, for example, kills replicants that he knows haven't committed any real crime, and who also reflect his own psychosis. Deckard is arguably also a replicant,

Deckard: A Philip Marlowe for 2019

probably a NEXUS 6, and so in essence one could argue that he is killing his own brothers and sisters.

Visually and stylistically *Blade Runner* has the look and feel of a film noir. The rain-soaked Los Angeles streets, the plot change from 'penthouse' apartments to inner-city hovels, the forties fashions, the long, dirty mac worn by Deckard, and the low-tech interiors and concrete brick exteriors of many of the buildings all recall the bleak setting and dress codes of a classic film noir pot boiler. The chiaroscuro (light and dark) lighting codes add to this effect. Shafts of light break through into dingy interiors and strike the sides of the characters' faces to suggest moral uncertainty or an embedded identity crisis. Deckard and Rachael first make love (although this starts out as a rape scene) in a low-key lit, sparsely furnished room, at the precise moment they are the least sure about one another. But this noir environment is also supported by parts of the Vangelis soundtrack: the saxophone blues solos that punctuate a number of the public/bar scenes reek of melancholy and loss.

However, there is another key reference point for the film in terms of its tortured look and overall down-beat mood – one that links film noir to German Expressionism and to Fritz Lang's *Metropolis* (1927). In German Expressionist films the 'mood-image' functions as a pathetic fallacy, as a way of suggesting the pessimism of the world and the alienation of the central characters. Off-centre framing, shadowy lighting techniques, distorted and wrongly sized city/townscapes, long shots with little cutting, and the use of acute angles, lines and perspectives are all used to create the impression of a creeping dystopia. The seminal expressionist image for a city without a soul is found in *Metropolis* – on the surface a mechanical, metal clad sea of hi-rises, but down below, beneath the ground, a slave camp where the faceless workers blindly operate the machinery for their rich masters. If one were to graft Los Angeles 2019 onto the city of Metropolis in some respects they would be a perfect fit.

Blade Runner as Police-Detective Story

The other generic stopping-off point for *Blade Runner*, and one related to film noir, is the police-detective drama. Deckard, the best Blade Runner there is, is called back into law enforcement to track down and 'retire' a number of escaped replicants. To do this he must follow clues, chase up leads, and solve a number of narrative enigmas along the way. To help Deckard in his pursuit of the replicants he has at hand the classic procedural and scientific tools to help him: a gun, (restricted) access to data and statistics, and a 'questioning' technique borne out of years of interrogation.

Deckard is evenly matched with his nemeses, and shares a number of their attributes. He is a world-weary anti-hero, messed up by years of killing people he identifies with. His investigation of the replicants is at the same time an investigation into his own psyche. Running alongside this primary plot is the central enigma of his and Rachael's identity – are they or are they not replicants? Is their love affair real, authentic, or itself made out of crisis and despair, one that is running out of literal and metaphorical time? In a police-detective story such puzzles run through the length of the film.

Blade Runner's Generic Hybridity

Generically speaking, *Blade Runner* is one of those films that mixes genres together – very like the 'patchwork' motif that Scott ascribes to the overall look of the film. As was noted before, hybridity is actually common place in Hollywood, especially in the age of the blockbuster aesthetic – a trend J. Hoberman (1985) attributes to *Star Wars*:

> Drawing on the western and the war film, borrowing motifs from fantasies as varied as *The Wizard of Oz* and *Triumph of the Will*, George Lucas pioneered the genre pastiche.

However, in *Blade Runner* the mixing of visual and narrative conventions from several genres is used to striking effect, acting, as it does, as an indicator of the film's nightmarish, dystopian agenda. By having the film situated symbolically in the past (through the low tech noirish aesthetics, the 'private eye' drama, and the pastiche of Mayan and Egyptian architecture) the future is made to look regressive – as if, paradoxically, the progress of science and technology has been a disastrous step backwards for humankind. Time hasn't stood still in the film but rather has, in many respects, gone back to earlier, grimmer periods of human existence.

However, the mixing of genres serves another purpose: it hints at or rather 'echoes' the confusion at the core of identity formation in the film, and gives texture to the schizophrenia that many of the characters display. Deckard is part jaded cop, loner, rebel, replicant, human, lover and rapist; and this type of character fracture best exists in a world that is not boundaried or fixed – a world made up or out of a mixture of styles that don't really belong together. Los Angeles 2019 is in one sense the embodiment of Deckard's psyche.

2. Narrative

Film Language

One of the most amazing properties of film is the way it crafts stories through its own distinct audio-visual language. Through the specific cinematic tools of lighting, shot choice, length and composition, sound, and editing; and through the overall arrangement of *mise-en-scène*, or what is put in to/in front of the frame, sealed worlds, with textured characterisation, emerge. *Blade Runner* is exemplary in its use of 'film language' since it crafts a complex and visually stunning story together with sublime artistry – a story in fact that because it coheres out of a hybrid mixture of genres is also like a Pandora's box of cinematic influences and references. In terms of cinematography, colour use, shot depth and distance, light and sound are used to create the impression that the future is both beautiful in its neon electrification and ugly in terms of its lower level miseries and despair.

In terms of lighting, characters can be rendered good, bad or duplicitous just through the use of coloured filters, gels and the amount and direction of light that falls onto them. Dark hues and low key light that catches just one side of a character's face forebodingly suggests that they are not to be trusted. Dr. Tyrell's first appearance in the film is coded in such a way and with his large lens glasses absorbing and reflecting light he appears as a devouring, all-consuming figure.

Chiaroscuro lighting heightens the noir ambience

The lighting of an environment works in a similar way: a world shot through with blues, greys and browns, and low level light help generate despair and suggest that this is a dystopian space. However, it is the bright artificial neon light that comes to be a haunting presence in *Blade Runner*. Light is everywhere in *Blade Runner*, reaching into every corner, every crevice of the *mise-en-scène* so that one cannot escape the 'searchlight' for a single second, one cannot find privacy for a moment. Of course, lighting codes can be used to fool an audience or to 'play' with their expectations. A character caught emerging from the shadows may be after redemption rather than plotting betrayal. One only has to think of Rachael in this respect – low-key lit like a devious *femme fatale*, and distrusted by Deckard, she ultimately becomes the embodiment of innocence and transcendence for the world-weary hero. Similarly, within the chaos of *Blade Runner* City there is radiant beauty to admire: the spinner's inaugural flight over Los Angeles 2019 is so captured that as it disappears into the glittering distance the 'glitter' washes over the spinner, as if it is merging in perfect unison with the electronic circuits of the city.

The glittering spinner, 'beautiful in its neon electrification'

Scott Bukatman (1997) attributes the tech-noirish feel of the film to the work of Jordan Cronenweth, the director of photography on the film:

> Cronenweth's characteristic method, especially on interiors, involved combining a soft frontlight (sometimes a soft uplight), with a hard backlight, creating intense silhouettes and haloes; the addition of smoke or reflective effects in the background further abstracted the space. The end results were crisp, even harsh, while remaining hazy and glamorous.

In terms of individual shots, the way a character or location is framed produces a great deal of textual meaning. A wide panoramic establishing shot of a luminous city situates the spectator in a particular time, place and location, and allows them to immediately recognise the importance of it to any likely future action. Blade Runner City isn't just a location – it is an agency of change and transformation, a place of power relationships and social inequalities that emerge from its materials, buildings and spatial arrangements. Deckard is being driven crazy by the city's internal logic of chaos.

In terms of individual characterisation a low angle medium shot allows a character to appear powerful and forceful, especially if it is cut straight after a high angle medium shot on what becomes the 'victim' in the scene. The power inequalities between Deckard and Batty are in part established in this way, in their final cat-and-mouse encounter. By contrast, de-centred and decanted framing produces a different effect: as if the viewpoint of the character is unstable or if the world that is being filmed is out of kilter. More generally, through attributed point-of-view (POV) shots (where we see what a character sees) and non-attributed point-of-view shots a more complete subjectivity enters the film, one that invites the spectator to identify with and 'enter' the fictional world that is being created.

The street scenes best encapsulate this type of subjectivity. Often shot with a hand-held camera the lower levels feel threatening, unstable, crowded and claustrophobic. When Deckard is in the scene this dislocated subjectivity appears to be his, or at least as belonging to his, in part poisoned, point of view. When Deckard is in pursuit of the other replicants the frenetic camerawork makes the chase kinetic and as charged as the neon signs that also fill the scene(s).

Deckard's pursuit of Zhora is 'as charged as the neon signs' in the scene

Diegetic sound (sound that emanates from the action that may be taking place both on and off screen) and non-diegetic sound (the film's musical score, soundtrack and mood music) complements the visual arrangements of the film. Sound is often synchronised and its sources are often rooted to the action that takes place on screen. A spinner rises off the ground, we hear the pull of the engine; a trigger on a gun is pulled, we hear the shot and the death rattle of the victim it hits. Similarly, the synth and blues score that magically strike up from nowhere are nonetheless connected to the images on screen because they carry on/over the mood of the scene – as if for all intents and purposes the drama of the scene has created the melodic sounds that we hear. Of course, sound works in a much more creative way in *Blade Runner* because, just as was the case with light, sound seems to be pouring out from everywhere, constantly invading what should be private, quiet moments. Dislocated (foreign, inaudible or muffled) voices, the pelt of rain, the buzz and hum of neon lights, engines purring, adverts proclaiming, trafficators instructing, the sound of the street crowd, market traders calling, all compete in a world of constant noise.

It is the grammar of the editing that invisibly stitches individual shots together to render a story truly meaningful and 'realistic'. Through eye-line matches, match cuts, adherence to the 180 degree rule (whereby 'the line' is never crossed in the editing of shots taken from different set-ups in a single location), and general continuity cuts between shots, action appears continuous in both time and space, mirroring, in one sense, the way spectators themselves experience the world. This realism effect is maintained because the editing process is effaced. As Annette Kuhn (1999) suggests:

> Continuity editing establishes spatial and temporal relationships between shots in such a way as to permit the spectator to read a film without any conscious effort, precisely because the editing is 'invisible'.

Continuity editing is also one of the central markers of the classical narrative produced within much of mainstream Hollywood cinema. However, as I now want to go onto argue, *Blade Runner* subverts a number of these 'classical' traditions.

Classical Narrative: Classical Hollywood Realism

Writers such as Bordwell and Thompson (2002) have argued that fiction films produced within the Hollywood studio system follow a pretty rigid narrative pattern, and tell their stories through a set narrative form. In fact, so coherent and consistent is this mode of storytelling that it can be given a name: *Classical Hollywood Realism*. *Blade Runner*, a studio picture and a genre film, is in many respects a Classical Hollywood film. However, at numerous points the film also subverts or problemitises this definition.

The Classical Hollywood film produces psychologically defined individuals, often in the shape of clear-cut heroes and villains, who are given 'goal' directed motivations. In *Blade Runner*, Deckard is the 'hero', given the task/goal of hunting down and retiring the replicants. We get to know him as an anxious, alienated, troubled character and empathy, as a consequence, builds up between him and the audience. Collectively, the replicants are the 'villains' and Roy Batty the arch-enemy – an apparently cold-blooded murderer on a revenge mission to wipe out his maker. Batty and Deckard get to slug it out in the classic end of film showdown.

However, if one looks again at the characterisation in the film, one can argue that the lines of good and evil are blurred. Batty, for example, saves Deckard from near-certain death, and so proves that there is humanity at the core of his cyborg being. The tyrannical Tyrell Corporation is arguably, by contrast, the real monster in the film, driven singularly by greed and commercial profit. In essence, *Blade Runner* blurs the lines between good and evil, and complicates audience identification.

The Classical Hollywood film tells its story through a singular protagonist or main causal agent. This protagonist is usually a male star, someone who has been marketed as a leading man. The protagonist is the target of any narrative restriction, although the audience can and often does know more than the protagonist in terms of clues given, and events that the protagonist may not directly witness. In *Blade Runner*, Deckard is the main protagonist: the vehicle through which the various events of the film are stitched together. It is his investigations that motor the film, and in the original release, his voice-over that provided the holistic and concluding commentary on what has taken place. Mostly in the film, Deckard's indecision is also the audience's, and they get to know something (like the fact that Rachael is a replicant) at the same time as Deckard does.

Harrison Ford, who plays Deckard, was becoming a huge Hollywood star on the back of the *Star Wars* and *Indiana Jones* franchises, and he brings this 'star image' to the part. However, one can argue that this is was what posed a problem for contemporary audiences of *Blade Runner*. Ford had been manufactured as a punch throwing, high octane, enigmatic action star. Deckard, by contrast, is an anti-hero, wracked with self-doubt and moments of indecision. He is literally on the edge of sanity in the film. We see him scared witless in his final encounter with Roy Batty. We see him act brutally and with a degree of cowardice: he shoots the fleeing Zhora in the back and is second place in his fight with Pris until he uses his gun. Most notably it is his misogynistic treatment of Rachael that is most striking: their first love-making scene is actually an enforced encounter. This dislocation or problematic fit between star image and role can be uncomfortable for audiences. However, the use of Ford in this way can also be read as a masterstroke by Scott because such dislocation adds to the sense of schizophrenia that permeates the film. Audiences are forced to read Ford/Deckard as if they are indeed in crisis.

In the Classical Hollywood film, the entire film world functions causally. All the elements that go into storytelling, from characterisation, *mise-en-scène*, sound and continuity editing, work as action and reaction or as cause and effect. All events happen for a purpose, and these events affect other events, and the world these events happen in contributes to all the outcomes. We have already established how sealed a world *Blade Runner* is, with its entire visual and narrative framework operating in a cause and effect manner.

However, it is the cause and effect nature of the Hollywood narrative that is of specific interest here. According to narrative pattern theories, Hollywood films generally begin in equilibrium: the film world that the audience enters into is in a state of harmony, where the social system works, and people are happy and contented. Images of plenitude are often present. Into this world an evil or disruptive force soon arrives, threatening by their very presence its stability. In turn, something specific (terrible) happens which turns this world upside down – a murder, rape, theft, etc. Grieving and mourning take place where the serious nature of the disorder is recognised. It is acknowledged that something has to be done. The main causal agent is assigned the task of making the world right again: he/she begins a lawful, sanctioned search, a quest to find and deal with the perpetrator(s). Along the way the causal agent encounters trial, tribulations, and false trails/idols but these serve to make the causal agent stronger and further validate the legitimacy of the quest. As the narrative progresses more and more of the puzzles and enigmas are solved or are brought to the point where they can only be resolved. The causal agent ends up in a situation where he/she directly confronts the evil force(s). Any remaining questions are answered including the question of motivation for the terrible deeds committed by the arch villain(s). The causal agent vanquishes the evil force(s) through strength, guile, skill and moral right. The film world is then brought back to a state of equilibrium or re-equilibrium, although things have had to change. The causal agent has been transformed by the quest, and the world of the film has been taught a powerful ideological message about moral responsibility. As the film ends, the narrative has been brought to close where all loose ends have been tied up.

In many respects, one can see straight away how *Blade Runner* subverts this type of narrative patterning. The momentary equilibrium the film starts with is already shot through with dystopian sentiments. Los Angeles 2019 is a terrible place *to begin with* – a futuristic vision of Dante's inferno with its burning oil towers and eternal nightscape. The arrival of the NEXUS 6 replicants to this world arguably brings a degree *more* 'humanity' to it, not less, since they are the one positive representation of the 'family' in the film. Their presence threatens no one apart from the corrupt tyrant Dr Tyrell, who fears for his own life, and the capital worth of his corporation.

Deckard reluctantly takes on the quest to hunt them down, or rather he is forced to take up the assignment, threatened with the removal of his cop privileges if he doesn't. His journey in the film is one of doubt and increasing confusion over who he is and what he is doing. The film arguably gets more ambiguous in terms of its morality the more it progresses. When Deckard confronts Batty at the end of the film he is not up to the task at hand – his quest has left him existentially adrift and he wants no more of killing. In a narrative twist, Batty saves Deckard's life allowing him (Batty) a more 'human' demise moments later. At this precise moment, identification arguably shifts from Deckard to Batty, or audience identification is at least shared between the two similarly constructed protagonists. By the end of the film some confusion reigns over whether Deckard is a replicant and this narrative enigma is left partially unresolved, signified only by a paper unicorn left by Gaff as if he has had access to what therefore must be Deckard's *implanted* dreams. The closure is itself shot through with sadness: Deckard and Rachael may have found love together but their time is short. Consequently, the ending is ultimately a depressing affair at least in relation to the Hollywood norm.

Anti-narrative Ambiguities

Another way of understanding *Blade Runner*'s narrative is in terms of the way it functions, in part, like the anti-narrative film found in a great deal of European art cinema. We have already noticed that one of the film's reference points is German Expressionism but the dislocated and open-ended nature of the narrative also more widely suggests a challenging art aesthetic borrowed from film movements such as the French New Wave. *Blade Runner*'s narrative is marked by gaps and enigmas that are never fully cohered or resolved (for example, the whereabouts of the fifth replicant is never revealed or explained during the film – is it Deckard himself?). Loose ends abound right up to the denouement when Deckard's replicant status is left unclear. There is a high degree of self-reflexivity and intertextuality in the film. The film self-consciously quotes from other film texts, art forms and media including the films *Metropolis*, *Double Indemnity*, *Mildred Pierce*, the science fiction comic *Heavy Metal*, and the artists Vermeer and Edward Hopper. This enables the film to be read in quite complex ways, well outside of the specifics of its classical narrative trajectory. In fact, so intimately and creatively visual is the film one can argue that it is less like a narrative than a moving picture painting.

A Visual Narrative

One of the arguments made about contemporary science fiction is that it is predominately driven by a desire to be *always* visually spectacular. Modern science fiction, so the argument runs, is purely a visual feast, a modern 'cinema of attractions' (Gunning, 1990), where the pleasure and the appeal of the genre reside in what it can show, what it can create with and through its special effects alchemy. And what it can create is the most unbelievable (but yet *diegetically* believable) spacecraft, futuristic cities, weapons, monsters and modes of inter-galactic transport, all conjured up in electrifying, digitally created action sequences. Modern science fiction is argued to be breathless, awe-inspiring, and wondrous *but only to look at*. What this argument presumes is that in the modern science fiction film, narrative is forsaken for the quick fix of a special effects shot or sequence, for the unremitting roller-coaster aesthetic that is presumed to drive all narrative events and outcomes. Modern science fiction tells lousy stories.

When one thinks of *Blade Runner* in this context, one can see how the film might be argued to be a visual feast, a spectacular film in terms of its futuristic cityscape *mise-en-scène*. In fact, if one goes back to the critical mauling the film got on its initial release, one can see a trend where the film is praised for its spectacular setting but is criticised for its incoherent and reductive/clichéd film noir plot. ('Muddled yet mesmerising' was how the *New York Times* (25 June 1982) described the film.)

Ridley Scott's own authorship is important here: with an award-winning background in advertising, where one only has 30 seconds to sell a product, making full use of visual imagery is central to transmit information quickly, the visual emphasis has come to dictate the way he researches and plans for the shoot. Scott goes to visual sources, right across the arts and mass media, to texture his storyboards, to affect the script, and his production designers are often the most renowned people working in the field (the artist H.G. Giger on *Alien* (1979), Syd Mead (an industrial designer credited as 'visual futurist') and production designer Laurence G. Paull in *Blade Runner*).

The special effects work of Douglas Trumbull is also important here since his visually spectacular creations for films such as *2001: A Space Odyssey* (1968) and *Close Encounters of the Third Kind* (1977) were used to great effect in putting together the tech-noirish cityscape of Los Angeles 2019. However, according to Scott Bukatman, Trumbull's work on *Blade Runner* was always more than surface level visual appeal since the cityscape affected the narrative in dynamic ways, and contributed to the confusion over how technology was to be understood or experienced in the film. While there is no elaborate, climactic special effects set-piece in *Blade Runner*, the effects actually assist in constructing the meaning and *mise-en-scène* of almost every scene. In Bukatman's conceit (1997), special effects and the visually spectacular have real and discernible narrative affects:

> Trumbull's effects are profound and contemplative, and in each film that features his work there is at least one sequence where the characters stare mutely at the marvels they behold. These spectacular fields ... testify to the sublimity of technology, an experience of its beauty infused with the anxiety that acknowledges its power.

Similarly, if one takes the time to examine the narrative of *Blade Runner* one actually finds a profound meditation on the nature of human existence. The ambiguous plot speaks to the confusion that the central characters feel in the film. The quotations to film noir, to other film genres/movements, and to past historical contexts add to the schizophrenic sentiments of the film. The classical battle between man (Deckard) and machine (Batty) is actually shown to be a battle about the machine-within 'man'kind as it races towards the digital and genetic age. As Bukatman (1997) argues:

> Most critics missed an overtly humanist side to the film – a clear indication as to what being human was and what it meant. *Blade Runner* was not a film designed to provide
> straightforward answers to these questions. Its
> dehumanised world … superficially blocked the very
> possibility of humanist survival, yet subtle signs of its
> existence echoed through the cacophony of the city.

3. Representation

Representation is a concept given to the way things, objects, places, people come to have meaning in the social world. When one represents something one is trying to give it definition, to make the 'thing' comprehensible to others of the same or similar culture, so that when representation takes place meaning between people has been generated. Representation involves using the shared signs and codes of various textual, oral and visual languages, signs and codes that widely circulate in the world at any one time. Presently, in our culture the visual sign of the 'dove' on a white flag refers to not only the bird but to the notion of peace. Representationally speaking, the dove acts as a symbol for/of peace. Meaning has been generated through the use of this sign.

Media representations generally involve power relationships – certain things, objects, places, people are constructed (stereotyped, mythologised) as Other, not normal, taboo, or bad to possess or be in contact with. These ideologically loaded representations usually manifest in sets of binary oppositions such as: man/woman; white/black; natural/synthetic; city/country; insider/outsider; heterosexual/homosexual. Audiences are asked to identify with only one side of these binaries, and to reject or oppose their counter-representations. In terms of a great deal of Hollywood cinema, audiences have been asked to identify with the morally right, white, heterosexual male, as against, for example, the deviant black or homosexual, and the active, independent woman.

Blade Runner is extremely interesting in terms of representation because while on the one hand many of these clearly defined binary oppositions are present, on the other there is also a high degree of blurring and disintegration between them. The key representational sites in *Blade Runner* coalesce around technophobia, the spatial organisation of the city, the politics of race, gender and the arena of the postmodern.

Technophobia and Technophilia

In *Blade Runner*, in one clear and direct sense the growth of technology has resulted in a future where nature and the natural has been nearly entirely snuffed out. Media technologies blast out from every street corner transmitting adverts, travel directions, warnings, news bulletins, whilst engaging in the most pervasive, all-seeing form of surveillance. There are very few private, technology free spaces in *Blade Runner* so that one is unable to be 'natural' because one is under constant watch. In fact, technology even invades one's dreams through memory implants (Deckard's dream of the unicorn dance being a key moment in the Director's Cut, revealing, as it arguably does, his replicant status). Techno-science has produced a superior form of human life in terms of the NEXUS 6 and bio-tech corporations rule, so it seems, the entire planet. Not only do unmarked cyborgs walk the city streets but cyberpets and genetically engineered life-forms populate people's homes (a concept more explicit in Philip Dick's source novel). Sky-rises pay homage to the most advanced form of civil engineering, and flying forms of transportation make all vertical and horizontal forms of space accessible and therefore crowded (or at least teeming with technology since, at times, Los Angles 2019 seems empty of people, at least on the upper levels). When Deckard is first taken up in the 'spinner', level after level of this technologically crowded metropolis is revealed like a never ending trail of signals and transmissions. Consequently, in this supra-mechanical Los Angeles 2019, not one blade of grass grows, not one glorious dawn rises, and not one natured landscape appears on the horizon. In essence, then, the film is deeply technophobic and pitches the technological against the natural in a relationship that calls out for the beauty of the country – precisely Rachael and Deckard's exit point in the original release of the film. Michael Ryan and Douglas Kellner (1990) argue that from a conservative perspective,

> technology represents artifice as opposed to nature, the mechanical as opposed to the spontaneous, the regulated as opposed to the free, an equaliser as opposed to a promoter of individual distinction, equality triumphant as opposed to liberty, democratic levelling as opposed to hierarchy derived from individual superiority.

However, *Blade Runner* does complicate the relationship between technology and nature somewhat, collapsing to a degree the binary opposition between them. In two key respects it is the technological in the film that is being validated or authenticated or at least humanised/naturalised in the film.

Pris and Batty may be replicants but their love is 'real'

First, the replicants – Deckard (perhaps), Rachael, Batty, Pris, Zhora, Leon – are all ultimately shown to be more fully human than many of the human characters we get to see in the film. Partly because they drive the narrative and we therefore get to know them more intimately than anyone else, and partly because they demonstrate a number of positive human qualities that we are all familiar with, they come to represent the *potential* of what happens when machine and human come together in unison. Dr. Tyrell, by contrast, has forgotten what it means to be human: in his pursuit for scientific knowledge and economic power he has become the one true unfeeling, arch-rationalist in the film – an embodied tyrannical machine. So, in one sense it is not that the binary opposites of (bad) technology verses (good) nature have been completely reversed, rather they have been collapsed in terms of the replicants (so that the harmony between man/nature and machine/technology is being potentially suggested as a positive here) but reinforced in terms of Dr. Tyrell (who has become more machine-like and consequently has forgotten what it means to be a good human in the face of commerce).

The replicants, in fact, are often the only ones in the film to be situated in contexts where human values and images of the natural are present. The rebel replicants are an imagined family unit, and the only extended family in the film. They look out for one another: they are immensely loyal to one another, embodying the cultural axiom that blood is thicker than water. In terms of the relationship between Batty and Pris there is shown to be real love there. By contrast, everyone else we encounter in the film exists as isolates; or as people who, we have to conclude, are from broken homes, since biological mothers and fathers are entirely absent; or as people looking, longing for love – Deckard and Rachael fit this latter model but the love they find together is not one between two human beings. Is it that in *Blade Runner* humans cannot fall in love anymore?

The religious iconography that circulates around Batty adds weight to the reading that the replicants are connected to a higher truth – are, by some miraculous conversion, the fallen but eventually redeemed ones in the film. Critic Robin Wood (1986) has noted how the replicants' impact is based on 'the multiple connotations they accrue as the film proceeds, through processes of suggestion, association and reference'. For example, Batty's introduction is accompanied by a near-quotation from William Blake's poem, *America: A Prophecy:*

> Fiery the angels fell; deep thunder rolled
> Around their shores, burning with the fires
> of Orc. (lines 115–16)

As Wood notes:

> Blake's poem is a celebration of the American Revolution, a narrative about the founding of modern America, interpreted on a spiritual/symbolic plane. Orc leads the revolt against oppression; he is one of Blake's devil-angles ... Roy, however, misquotes: Blake's original reads 'Fiery the angels *rose*' ... The change from 'rose' to 'fell' must be read, then, in terms of the end of the American democratic principle of freedom, its ultimate failure...

Further, Batty dies an implicitly religious, Christ-like death: dressed in a loin-cloth he 'saves' Deckard from an early/earthly death, puts a nail through his palm, and at the moment of his own death he releases a white dove into the heavens – peace, at last, for the man without a real earthly Father (or Mother, as I will shortly go onto argue).

Second, *Blade Runner* also has clear elements of *technophilia* or a love for showing and displaying the operations and functions of the technological as it impacts on everyday life in Los Angeles 2019. Visually, in amongst the smog and burning oil fires there is a luminous beauty that emanates from the neon signs, advertising blimps, the mechanical toys, the spinners and trafficators and the re-engineered Mayan and Egyptian edifices. *Blade Runner* is, to repeat an earlier argument, wonderful to look out, conjured up from state-of-the-art special effects, and one that in part creates an awe of/for the technologies used to texture this future world.

Batty, 'burning with the fires of Orc'

This barely concealed technophilia is also due to Ridley Scott's 'layering' effect where the *mise-en-scène* of the film has been composed with varying textures in mind. If one takes these layers/textures to be technology based or inflected, then the look, feel and impressions of technology saturate the entire filmworld and consequently the experience one gets from watching the film. Of course, looking, being seen, watched, or not seeing what is really there is central to the film's narrative trajectory and subject positioning. These technologies of seeing – electronic eyes, scanning devices, photographic cameras, retina devices, etc. – are everywhere in the film and they produce a layered gaze or a type of miraculous vision. When one looks or is looked at (penetrated) in the film there is a beauty to the gaze employed but this is ultimately a terrifying beauty that one cannot escape from – a simultaneous technophobic/technophiliac beauty.

In *Blade Runner*, the viewer is drawn into the film's affective economy because the screen 'expresses a "human-like" mode of perceptual consciousness: the camera and microphones articulate a technologically inflected version of what a human body in that situation might experience' (Stadler 202: 240). In a phenomenological or experiential sense, the viewer *becomes one* with the film because 'we are part of the film, joined in hermeneutic and embodiment relations with it in inseparable symbiosis' (Stadler, 2002, 241).

The Crumbling City

The futuristic cityscape has always been one of the key iconic signs of the science fiction film and a central device for representing social division and power relationships between people. The city emerges as an 'affective power ... a specific power to affect both people and materials – a power that modifies the relations between them' (Sobchack, 1999). In *Metropolis*, for example, the mechanised work routines that take place in underground concrete factories, where no natural light shines, produce compliant, herd-like workers. These workers are in effect brain dead from the monotony of their alienated labour and are turned into prisoners because of the prison-like architecture they are contained within. This spatial arrangement affects them at their core so that they become less than human in their less than human/natural surroundings.

In *Blade Runner* the city works to instil a pervasive sense of alienation and loss, and to shape and define the motivations of the characters that live there. Los Angeles 2019 is largely an urban nightmare – a nightmare fleshed out of the materials of globalisation, capitalism, cyberpunk, and noir, so that its neon and concrete veins and arteries appear clogged up and yet leaky, pouring despair onto its inhabitants. According to Scott Bukatman (1997), cyberpunk is one of the key references for the film's representation of the urban because of its high-tech yet exhilarating chaos, set at street level, and because of the centrality of media/cyber communication to its imaginings,

> *Blade Runner*'s cyberpunk urbanism exaggerates the presence of the mass media, evoking sensations of unreality and pervasive spectacle: advertising 'blimps' cruise above the buildings, touting the virtues of the off-world colonies, and gigantic vid-screens dominate the landscape with images of pill-popping geishas.

Nobody appears to be home/at home in Los Angeles 2019. Along the lower levels population flows happen in tidal proportions, and people move like rats in a sewer, as various communication signs direct behaviour from one boundary-less destination to another. Along these rain- and neon-soaked corridors of decay and endless consumption, punks rub shoulders with Buddhist monks and debutantes and other marginal groups and outsiders. Spatially, the inner city appears to stretch out horizontally forever, so that it is only through vertical orientation that suburbia can be reached – in essence, the higher up one lives the higher one's social standing or economic position. Suburbia is high in *Blade Runner* while the inner city low.

Deckard has let the city get (in)to him, or rather Deckard is the city and the city is (within) him: he is plugged directly into its electronic veins and arteries, once again confirming, through association, his status as a replicant. And just like the city is in a state of perpetual dementia so is Deckard in a state of existential crisis. However, the symbiotic relationship between Deckard and the city is much more complex, because it is a relationship that returns us once again to the argument that the nature/technology binary opposition is blurred in the film.

Los Angeles 2019 is an ugly/beautiful technological city – it reeks of mediated decay and cyber loneliness and loss (its technophobic inflection) but it also speaks of progress and contains shards of enlightened practices (its technophilia inflection). The city seems to have expunged all traces of the natural and yet water, rain and tears remain a constant presence in the film, and connect an albeit polluted 'nature' to/with the replicants. In short, there is good to be had in this technological city and nature still finds its way into the darkest corners of its spatial planes. Similarly, Deckard is an ugly : beautiful man – worn through from the inside out, he nonetheless pursues the replicants because of his pre-programmed duty to retire them. He almost *automatically* rapes Rachael in their first sexual encounter. At the same time, the pain of all this killing is getting to him and he questions his/their place in the social order – such humanist principles are getting in the way of his rationalist/mechanical 'instincts'. The more the film progresses, the more he doubts himself, the technological system, and he expresses fear and loathing in equal measure. Deckard the replicant is becoming more techno-human by the day, and in terms of the film's overriding ideological position, this is a pretty good thing because it serves to challenge the binary oppositions of man/machine and the unequal power relationships that have stemmed from this.

Los Angeles 2019 – an ugly : beautiful place

'Ridleyville', the nickname given to the major set used to create Los Angeles 2019, was designed at the Warner Bros. Burbank Studios, originally the setting for a great number of detective and noir films made during the studio system (from the 1930s onwards). Allied to the film's design practice of 'retrofitting' or 'upgrading old machinery or structures by slapping new add-ons to them' (Mead quoted in Sammon, 1996) to create the cityscape, one gets a sense of how central the past was to the futuristic look of the film. Scott immersed himself in a wider set of visual sources: 'engravings by Hogarth and paintings by Vermeer, photographs by Jacob Riis of New York's Lower East Side, the urban nightdreams of Edward Hopper and the baroque visual science fiction of *Heavy Metal*' (Bukatman, 1997).

However, it is the real and representational city of New York that most influences the cityscape of Los Angeles 2019. The urban sprawl, the congestion and density of people and buildings and the impression that things are grinding to a desperate halt all echo sentiments made about New York before and at the time of the film's release. As Scott himself said, 'you go into New York on a bad day and you look around and you feel this place is going to grind to a halt at any minute' (quoted in Sammon, 1996). *Metropolis* is of course central to the connection here since Fritz Lang based his futuristic city on the skylines and vertical and horizontal lines of the New York that he experienced during a visit there. *Blade Runner*, then, in a complex line of intertextuality, gets to New York through German Expressionism, a fabricated Los Angeles, and black and white documentary style photographs.

Class Pathology

In one direct way, one can make the link from *Blade Runner*'s representation of the 'working class' back to a particular type of British social realist film in which, in particular, working class men are stereotyped as misogynist, non-communicative brutes, and working class spaces are marked out as pathological. In films such as *Kes* (1969), *Rita, Sue, and Bob too* (1986), *Naked* (1993), and *Nil By Mouth* (1997), the 'ghetto' areas that the films are largely set in literally produce men whose violence, drug addiction, alcoholism and criminality seem to stem from the lack of space, the lack of status that such environments carry with them. Two pivotal, recurring metonymic shots from these films concretise this. The first shot is an exterior, low-lit pan across hi-rose council flats, or back-to-back terraces, on a dull day. The shot suggests that life is drab here, and the lack of natural colours and the absence of organic textures (such as trees, green fields or even grass) extends the metaphor that this is a harsh, unforgiving, concrete jungle that will/does swallow up its inhabitants. The second shot, a continuity cut, is an interior shot, supposedly within one of these flats or houses, where families are arguing, abusing one another or are engaging in illegal acts. The interior lacks natural light, is poorly decorated and is over-crowded, with too many people living together in such a small space. The working class men in these spaces are found to drink too much, quarrel too much, fight and fuck too much, and they resort to domestic violence to deal with their social/economic inadequacies.

In *Nil By Mouth* we are presented with a variation of this: an interior shot of one of the central protagonists stealing dope from his brother-in-law is followed by two exterior shots of what we presume to be these council flats on a dull, colourless night. The harsh vertical and horizontal lines of the blocks of flats 'slash' each of the frames and, because the camera remains still, again in both shots, there is a complete absence of the organic, the natural, to the representation. When the camera cuts back to the interior again, the brother-in-law appears and proceeds to actually bite the nose of the 'thief' – a family member. In this hostile environment, the film's representation of working-class men is as nothing more/less than animals.

Blade Runner uses the exterior pan in a similar way, but not only for self-contained lower level spaces such as that encountered in the 'purge' scene, but for the entire city, repeatedly photographed in long shot as a sprawling, heavy metal, Dante's Inferno. However, there is a third type of shot common to British social realism and *Blade Runner*. In films such as *Vroom* (1988), a space is created between the suffocating claustrophobia of the working class ghetto and the 'semi-rural'. A character emerges from the city to stand on a hill and look back at what he has just left behind, a shot 'emblematic of the desire to escape the confines of the city' (Hill, 1999: 169). Similarly, Deckard is able to look back on/at the city, not only in the police spinner he travels in, but from his apartment above the lower-levels. When Deckard looks out across the city, what he sees is a terrible confusion, a confusion that he feels at the core of his own dislocated (working class) being, and a longing for a permanent way to escape this God-awful place.

Race Relations

Wherever one looks in *Blade Runner* one will find issues of racial identity and racial difference projected onto the inhabitants, the city spaces, and the overall ideological message of the film. In one sense the film appears deeply racist, reproducing negative images of the East/the Orient and the racialised Other, while at the same time validating white identity or 'whiteness' over and above this 'yellow peril' or white-but-black slave simulacra. However, in another sense, *Blade Runner* appears to criticise white identity and to collapse racial distinctions, so that its racial politics emerge as positive, and in terms of mainstream Hollywood cinema, finally transgressive.

In *Blade Runner* there is a definitive 'Eastern' inflection given to the architecture and teeming hoards who populate the lower levels or the symbolic ghetto or inner city area of Los Angeles 2019. As Richard Dyer (1997) observes,

> Not unfriendly, not the enemy ... they are none the less portrayed within the racist discourse of the yellow peril: busy with their small enterprises, hard to communicate with, and there in their millions.

The replicant Zhora embodies much of this Eastern Othering in terms of ethnic hue, Eastern sounding name, and her eroticised, sexualised role. When Deckard catches up with her she is working as a snake dancer in a strip-club decorated with Egyptian motifs and populated by exotic animals. Her violent death soon after, shot through the back by Deckard, is quick and deadly retribution for her rebellion, aggressive sexuality and racial uncertainty, together acting as an embodied threat to white patriarchy – to Deckard's shaky white masculinity, in fact. In this reading Deckard functions as a crisis driven white male who has seen *his* town, *his* neighbourhood taken over by swarms of immigrants who have rejected the values of the American way. He is a white man adrift, driven to existential rage about the imagined/ potential/actual loss of his privileged position in the world.

The imbedded racialised nature of the replicants are important here: their role as slaves to mining corporations and leisure industries Off-world suggest a historical and metaphoric connection to black slaves of the American past – taken against their will from Africa and sold on as commodities to their new 'new world' masters. The replicant's attempt to pass as humans on earth echo the black person's, particularly mulatto, attempt to pass as white, so that they can each walk the earth free of persecution. In *Blade Runner*, it is arguably Deckard who does this passing best of all – but of course, he is not sure of where he comes from anyway.

Zhora's racial uncertainty and aggressive sexuality is a threat to the white, masculine world embodied by Deckard

This type of racial coding is structured into the very spatial organisation of the film so that people of race populate the lower levels of the city, while the white people live in the higher levels, or have moved Off-world all together, abandoning a city/planet that they see as having been taken over by the racial other. As David Desser (1999) argues, in relation to what he calls the film's high/low spatial metaphor:

> The replicants and the people of colour inhabit the teeming, rain-soaked streets ... highest of all, though, resides Eldon Tyrell, technocrat extraordinaire and Master of LA's metropolis, in a pyramid some seven hundred storeys high.

However, the racial coding may work through in a more progressive way in the film, particularly in relation to the replicants. Given that three of the four replicants are distinctly white, and in the case of Batty and Pris hyper-white, their metaphoric connection to slavery may actually work to remove the 'natural' connection between race and slavery that has been made by racist thinkers. Slavery in *Blade Runner*'s conjunction becomes a political operation, one based on power monopolies rather than some natural or essential condition that emanates from one's skin colour. *Blade Runner* meditates on the nature of slavery, deconstructing its racial antecedents.

Finally, there may actually be a barely concealed critique of what it means to be white in the film. White people are connected to technology and to (techno)science in the film so much so that people like Tyrell have been taken over by their/its rationalist, machine-like calculations. It is as if, if one becomes too concerned with the rational – if one becomes *too white* – then one is somehow *lacking*, in life or emotion. Given that Batty is the embodiment of hyper-whiteness, and Deckard is the world-weary white male supposedly on the run from people of colour (or is it his own lifeless whiteness?), death (or, more accurately, a lack of life) seems to hover over both of them. It is as if their cyborg status is a metaphor for white identity – something that is ultimately a form of nothingness, an absence, one that has become so lifeless that it reads as a pre-programmed death sentence for those who possess it. No wonder Batty wants 'more life, fucker'.

Gender Trouble

The sexual politics of *Blade Runner* seem to be on one level aggressively heterosexual and decidedly misogynistic. The three central female characters in the film operate within a field of vision that establishes their 'to-be-looked-at-ness' (Mulvey, 1989) and a narrative that punishes their independence. Rachael, Pris and Zhora are in different ways eroticised, fetishised and subjected to point-of-view shots that reduce them to fully realised objects of beauty or to a series of fractured bodily parts, with shots of their legs, faces, eyes, torsos dominating the way we come to see them. Rachael, the archetypal *femme fatale*, seductively enters the film dressed in high heels, a sharp, tight business suit and is framed in low key light but with a halo effect around her. She paradoxically appears to be both a Madonna and a Whore type figure – dark and light at the same time. In this 'interrogation' scene, Rachael visually speaks the language of female sexual danger, literally and metaphorically blowing smoke rings around Deckard as he seeks to discover her true identity. But she also comes to be seen as pure, untouched, wanting only to be loved by Deckard. It is as if the film can only deal with her (or any woman) in terms of these two essentialised feminine tropes – bad woman/good woman. Pris, the 'pleasure model' or prostitute, enacts her fetishised role in fish net tights, short skirt and near see-through top, and therefore appears to be mere 'eye-candy' for the male spectator. She seduces the innocent Sebastian only so that the replicants can gain access to Tyrell. Zhora, who takes work as an exotic dancer under the guise of Miss Salome, is, as we have seen, the embodiment of Othered female sexuality and her flight from Deckard, through the city streets, dressed only in a see-through 'dirty' mac and knee length boots, is arguably meant to foreground her wanton ways and to give justification to the bullet she receives in the back.

The misogyny in the film is situated with this type of violence being metered out on all the female characters. Deckard cruelly proves to Rachael that she is a replicant by recalling to her two of her most precious memories (memories that have actually been implanted by Tyrell without her knowledge). The masculine/feminine knowledge/power inequalities here leave her violated and distraught, and Deckard appears to gain some pleasure from this. Such violation takes a more perverse turn later on in the film when Deckard forces her to make love to him. This initially brutish encounter, although it very quickly becomes consensual, suggests that not only do women need heterosexual love to be complete, but coercion is a 'likeable', permissible or necessary part of the experience.

Of course, another way the film dismisses women is through their *absence*: men drive the narrative of *Blade Runner*. Men invent, detect, build and destroy in *Blade Runner*. Men make history in *Blade Runner*. Men provide the real heroes and villains in *Blade Runner*. Women, by contrast, simply provide the romantic interest and the sexualised body that is in part coded to be enjoyed as sexual spectacle by what are imagined to be male spectators. But not entirely; because these female bodies are often wayward bodies (*too* sexual, *too* promiscuous) they have to be punished or be put back into place within what is a patriarchal order within the film. This is why both Pris and Zhora die such brutal deaths. In short, *Blade Runner* suggests that patriarchy is natural and any challenges to this need to be put down or, to use the language of the film, be 'retired'.

However, one particular aspect of women's absence from the film is constructed as troubling. There are not any 'real' biological mothers in the film and it is this absence that forces Dr. Tyrell to invent memories for his replicants so that they can imagine that they were really born to/of a human mother. This is because without mothers, without mother nature or the nurturing, loving qualities of a good mother, replicants are themselves shown to be incomplete, confused, uprooted and ultimately dangerous as a result of this primal absence. It is precisely the terror of not having a mother which haunts Leon, Deckard and Rachael's memories, dreams and photographs. In fact the whole narrative of *Blade Runner* can be read as an Oedipal trajectory. Batty and his band of replicants return to earth in search of their origins. They want to return to or revisit that mythical, magical moment when they were at one with their mothers, close to the mother's breast and therefore safe, warm and complete. If they can return to mother then they can prove themselves to be human and not artificial (*man*-made). They will have proved that they really have lived. But Father (Dr. Tyrell) has intervened: mother has been destroyed, or rather has never really existed, and it is his word as God (originator) that goes. This is the law of the Father. The replicants do not have mothers and as such cannot find wholeness, tranquillity, and as a consequence their real 'lack' means they must be destroyed. The ideological message embedded here suggests that mother/motherhood is essential to a healthy, normal identity, and without *her* the world and its people would/has turn(ed) to chaos and dust.

However, one can also read the gender politics in the film in a more positive or progressive way. Rachael, Pris and Zhora can be said to destabilise gender categorisation in at least two clear ways. First, the excessively constructed nature of their femininity draws attention to it as construction or as artifice and performance. In particular, the self-reflexive Rachael, who consciously draws on the codes and conventions of the 1940s noir *femme fatale*, seems to be 'playing' with her Madonna/Whore identity; playing, at least initially, with the relatively weak Deckard and with the audience through a series of intertextual nods and winks. She is arguably an active and dynamic character with a high degree of knowing representational power. In general, these representations of excess (women as too sexual, too promiscuous) may actually be liberating from a feminist perspective because not only is patriarchy challenged in the film, but this challenge can also be extremely pleasurable for female spectators who want to throw off the repressive regimes of control that impact on their everyday lives by taking on, at least through identificatory practices, the 'wanton' ways of the central female characters.

Second, the cyborg origins of the central female (and male) characters destabilise the masculine/feminine binary oppositions found in the film precisely because they draw attention to the lie of the essentialist position – that the differences between men and women are biological, true across time. Replicants, because they are artificially made, draw attention to the fact that such gender distinctions can no longer be viewed as organic or natural but synthetic and manufactured. Men and women are literally 'made-up' in the film and as such human identity is shown to be always a matter of becoming rather than some fixed and rooted certainty. Of course, this is exactly what postmodernists refer to as 'identity crisis'.

Rachel: a femme fatale *for 2019*

The Postmodern in *Blade Runner*

> The postmodern aesthetic of *Blade Runner* is thus the result of recycling, fusion of levels, discontinuous signifiers, explosion of boundaries, and erosion. The disconnected temporality of the replicants and the pastiche city are all an effect of a postmodern, post-industrial condition: wearing out, waste. (Bruno, 1990)

Blade Runner is an exemplary postmodern text in the sense that it both represents the conditions of postmodernity and employs elements of the postmodern condition to texture its narrative. In its form, content, and ideological centre *Blade Runner* explores and utilises the strategies of quotation, pastiche, recycling, hyperreality and identity crisis. *Blade Runner* is a schizophrenic film, one that confuses history, mixes up traditions, collapses the differences between the real and the mediated, and as such supposedly articulates what it is like to live in the postmodern world we are all a part of.

Textually, *Blade Runner* quotes from different film genres and film movements/ periods, as well as from other visual media and actual historical periods – although these feel as if they have themselves been 'quoted' or lifted from post-cards, travel books and old films. In terms of the film's visual and narrative aesthetic *Metropolis*, *Mildred Pierce*, the New York skyline, the pulp fiction of Raymond Chandler, and the pages of the science fiction comic *Heavy Metal* are juxtaposed against Roman and Greek columns, neon lit Chinese dragons, Chinatown, Egyptian and Mayan pyramids and palaces. Consequently, time, history, high/low culture and the relations and differences between them have been thrown into confusion. *Blade Runner* happens in a future but one which is an amalgam of numerous pasts, and where taste distinctions have been levelled out. The film's central characters struggle to find a home in this leaky city, touched as they are by its boundary-less references and (im) possible subject positions. When Deckard looks out across the city what he sees is a terrible confusion, a confusion that he feels at the core of his own dislocated cyborg/ human being.

This is a tiresome confusion produced by a general aesthetic of decay. The constant streams of recycling in the film refer to both a lack of invention and renewal but also to generalised waste – the real waste produced by the architects of this endless recycling and the metaphoric waste or the wasting away of humanity produced by this hyperreal city. Los Angeles 2019 is full of waste: the refuse (ethnic minorities?) that clogs up the streets of the lower levels; and technological waste, in terms of the dystopian uses it has been put to (surveillance, consumption, pastiche), and the mis-use of the replicants – who literally waste away as slaves on Off-world colonies. These vestiges of waste, then, are also shot through with melancholy and regret – infused with a forlorn sensibility – buildings, roads, sidewalks, people, replicants seem to weep (often literally because of the rain) in *Blade Runner*. And the Vangelis soundtrack gives sonic, electronic texture to such melancholy.

Technology fuels this crisis because it has come to represent the difference between the real and the simulated in the film. In effect reality itself comes to be questioned or arguably vanishes in(to) the dislocated reflections of video screens, blimps, trafficators and memory implants. In *Blade Runner* the media is such an omnipresent force that it becomes the reality indicator – more real than real itself. For example, we never get to see the Off-world colonies sold to us in the film: they appear only as advertising signs – signs, therefore, without a concrete referent. Whether they exist or not – the exploits of the replicants suggest they do – is irrelevant because it is only the media sign that truly has significant ontological weight in the film.

In *Blade Runner* there is an overarching and insipid postmodern identity crisis that seems to touch everything and everyone in the film. Los Angeles 2019 is in a state of perpetual crisis. Composed of a patchwork of styles and fads it has no geographical centre, no 'original' past to refer to, no secure history to be bound to, and no concrete present to allow communities to foster. In one sense this is why the replicants, including Deckard, are drawn to its quarters – they share, imitate, and can plug into its schizophrenic state. But the relationship or correspondence is one borne out of the most despairing search for wholeness – all anyone (good) really wants in the film is a place, a history, a biography to call their own.

The world weary Deckard best represents this: his goal driven pursuit of the replicants and his love affair with Rachael are really a journey into his own (cyborg) heart of darkness. His real quest is a quest to discover his origins, to find the truth about who he really is and where he comes from. Of course, in *Blade Runner*, there is no privileged site of the real and so the ambiguity that remains over Deckard's identity is an ambiguity produced by a world entirely made up from simulation. In fact, perversely, Deckard, made of simulation, is more real than the human Tyrell, in the messed up hyperreal of Los Angeles 2019. Deckard is home but he nonetheless feels desperately homeless.

Blade Runner's postmodern aesthetic supposedly refers the audience back to the way the real world (our world) has developed. The film's technophobic elements echo (or in fact contribute to) the fears that technology and science have come to have too much influence and control over people's everyday lives – so much so in fact that what it means to be human is shifting as genetic engineering and artificial reproduction begin to remove people from the 'natural' origins of their species. The film's concern with mediation, and mediated technology works to articulate the condition that one increasingly experiences the real world second-hand, via terminals, video screens and television sets. The global and consumption perspectives of *Blade Runner* speak to the growth of trans-national corporations and the conceit that the world is now one global village – a village trading in goods and wares. Finally, the film's racial coding speaks to the rise of the Asian tiger economies and immigration flows – a western fear of swamping and of a loss of economic and political power to the 'yellow peril' of Sony and Honda. In sum, *Blade Runner* offers us a pretty bleak view of the present.

Blade Runner may also offer us a complex entry point for considering the post-human, defined as a new cybernetic creation born of a technological environment in which reality is essentially composed of information patterns. Deckard, for example, often seems to be merely one more electronic circuit plugged into a gigantic info-world of virtual merchandising, travel, advertising and news gathering. The post-human throws into confusion human/machine, natural/synthetic and mind/body dualisms, opening up the self to multiplicities.

4. Institutions and Authors

Blade Runner is arguably a textbook case of how the contemporary Hollywood studio system works – or rather fails to work properly. It is a case study of budgetary problems, falling outs, rows on the shoot, sneak screenings, sackings, final cuts, director's cuts, and how, at least initially, the commercial is privileged over all other artistic and professional considerations where film-making is concerned.

Trouble on the Shoot

On the back of the commercial success of *Alien*, Ridley Scott was considered to be a relatively 'hot property' in terms of the premiere league of film-makers working in Hollywood at the time. His near *auteur* status allowed him to pick the projects he wanted to work on, and financial backing was seemingly readily available for a film with his name on it. With this in mind, once *Alien* was finished he was given the opportunity of directing a big-budget version of Frank Herbert's sci-fi novel *Dune*. However, after working on it for several months he decided to drop out, fearful of how much time it would take him to complete. This eventually led him to taking on the *Blade Runner* project.

Blade Runner was offered to Scott by the producer Michael Deeley, whose most notable previous success had come with *The Deer Hunter* (1978) a film that had received the Academy Award for Best Picture. Deeley had secured a production budget of $13 million through Filmway Pictures, 'a mid-tier company that had absorbed and arisen from the corpus of the recently disbanded American-International Pictures, haven of drive-in schlock and Roger Corman classics' (Sammon, 1999). Scott officially signed on to make the re-named *Blade Runner* (originally titled *Dangerous Days*) on 21 February 1980. Trouble began soon after.

Blade Runner is based upon Philip K. Dick's novel *Do Androids Dream of Electric Sheep?* However, it was Hampton Fancher's screenplay that attracted Ridley Scott to the project:

> I was drawn to the moral content of his screenplay. Its central conceit was the
> idea of an officially sanctioned killer murdering what were, after all, really people
> ... I was also fascinated by the script's graphic possibilities ... *Dangerous Days*
> seemed to present the possibility of doing what I called 'layering' back then, the
> building up of carefully chosen details to create a fully imagined world. (quoted in
> Sammon, 1999)

However, before principal photography could begin, Scott set about working with
Fancher on ways to improve the plot, and texture the environment that the film
would take place in. Fancher produced eight separate drafts of the script but each
time Scott was unhappy, complaining that Fancher couldn't 'see' Los Angeles 2019.
This was compounded by Philip K. Dick's initial reaction to the script: 'I read two
drafts of Fancher's screenplay, both bearing the Filmways imprint, and it was just
one terrible script. Corny, extremely maladroit throughout' (quoted in Sammon,
ibid). Scott asked Fancher to look at the pages of the sci-fi comic *Heavy Metal* to
get a better sense of the way he wanted the world of *Blade Runner* to work/look
but this produced even more acrimony between them. The conflict got even worse
until Fancher was replaced by David Peoples, who would later go on to script the
Oscar-winning *Unforgiven* (1992). Peoples is credited with 'tightening the mystery
aspects of the screenplay and deepening the humanity of the android adversaries'
(Bukatman, 1997) Such struggles, unfortunately, would become a defining feature of
the whole production history of the film.

In the early days of the filming Scott clashed with Jordan Cronenweth, his director of
photography, over how to light the first scene in the film. Re-shooting had to take
place and consequently production fell behind schedule, and production costs went
up. This in turn meant that by December 1980 Filmways, who had financial problems
following a number of box-office flops, decided to drop *Blade Runner* from its
production schedule, fearful that the budget would go sky-high. This momentarily left
the film without financial backing. Meanwhile, on set, Harrison Ford and Sean Young
weren't getting on, and Ford was also resistant to Scott's directing methods, accusing
him of not being interested in the craft of acting. However, the biggest struggle
happened between Scott and his production crew. As Sammon (1999) summarises:

Blade Runner was the first film Scott had shot in Los Angeles under the strict, sometimes byzantine mandates of the American film unions; one such dictum forbade him to act as his own camera operator. Scott bristled at this restriction, calling such regulations 'illogical, like taking Arnold Palmer's golf clubs away from him'.

Overall Scott was having an awful time making the film – an experience he later compares to being on the ropes in a boxing match. This was compounded by the behaviour of the production companies who had come in to finance the film after the withdrawal of Filmways. Deeley had managed to broker a re-negotiated, three-way partnership deal between The Ladd Company, a subsidiary of Warner Bros., Sir Run Run Shaw, the Hong Kong cinema mogul, and American film and television production company, Tandem Productions, owned by producer Jerry Perenchio, writer/director Bud Yorkin, and director Norman Lear. The new deal had an increased budget of approximately $28 million with agreed domestic distribution rights for The Ladd Company, foreign distribution rights for Sir Run Run Shaw, and ancillary rights for Tandem productions. It was, however, Tandem Production's role as completion bond guarantor on the film that set the tone for the final battle over the film's direction.

Not The Final Cut

As soon as Tandem came on-board there were problems. As Bukatman (1997) summarises:

> Yorkin and Perechino (Lear was not involved with *Blade Runner*) had little confidence in the vision of the film's creators, especially as the production fell increasingly behind schedule ... It's also very possible that Tandem was beginning to realise that they had not funded an action-adventure of the order of *Star Wars*. The financial backers were increasingly upset about Scott's on-set perfectionism, which revealed itself in seemingly endless retakes.

Tandem put Yorkin in overall control of the film and this produced a situation where Scott was being constantly questioned about the direction the film was taking. Scott, in turn resented such interference and relations on and off set plummeted:

> But by the time I got into my third film, *Blade Runner*, I was again questioned so
> often about everything I did or wanted to do that the situation really pissed me off.
> That's when I became a screamer. I simply got fed up answering stupid questions.
> (quoted in Sammon, 1999)

By the time the film got to the editing stage, Tandem decided to fire Scott and
Deeley (although what this really did was make more concrete who was actually in
overall charge of the film, and anyway Scott and Deeley were quickly re-instated).
When the film was given a limited test screening in early March 1982 it was very
badly received with audiences offering a concerted critique of its confusing plot, slow
pace and ambiguous and dour ending. It was at this stage that Tandem wrestled
complete control of the film away from Scott and Deeley, demanding the two
now infamous changes to the film's structure: the addition of Deckard's voice-over
narration to 'glue' the film together, and the enforced happy ending where Deckard
and Rachael escape to the country at the same time as Deckard narrates the utopian
lines that she has in fact no termination date. When *Blade Runner* was released on
the 25 June 1982 it was met with much critical derision and very poor box-office. But
this is really only the first part of the institution story.

*Harrison Ford became
resistant to Ridley Scott's
direction*

The Director's Cut

The whole production context for the making of *Blade Runner* works as an excellent case study for considering the thorny issue of *film authorship*. On the one hand, the finished film clearly emerges from the collective efforts of the entire ensemble working on the film and not, therefore, just from the visionary hands of the director or *auteur*. Fancher and Peoples' script(s), Mead and Trumbull's special effects and production work, Cronenweth's photography, and the collectivised hands of the unionised production crew, all have a major influence on the final look and form of the film. Similarly, the generic codes and conventions of the science fiction film, and the numerous production constraints imposed on the film (principally by Tandem Productions), suggest a film borne out of media culture and the economics of commercial film production. Scott's contribution to this creative mix, while being very important, is not or cannot be over determining in these contexts.

However, one can also make a strong case for arguing that *Blade Runner* actually demonstrates how a visionary director or *auteur* puts their unique mark on the film in spite of these generic and production constraints, and precisely because they can cohere the efforts of a group of working people until their vision for the film has been realised. In this respect Scott seems an almost exemplary *auteur*. As Michael Deeley notes:

> It was really Ridley who generated and created or filtered the overall look of the picture ... I know film is a collaborative medium, and I certainly don't say this to take anything away from the hard work everyone else gave to the picture. But it was really Ridley Scott who designed *Blade Runner*. (quoted in Sammon, 1999)

It was Scott who researched and drew together the disparate elements of film noir, German Expressionism, realist urban photography, *Heavy Metal* science fiction and art, for his scriptwriters and production designers to work to; it was Scott – a trained artist – who produced reams of sketches to 'direct' the vision of the writers, wrist artists and special effect and set designers; it was Scott who took literal control of the shoot, lining up shots, demanding endless retakes, multi-tasking in each of the main areas of the shoot; and it was Scott who would snap, 'this is the way I want it – just do it' (quoted in Sammon, 1999). *And it was Scott*, finally, who would be given back a degree of authorial ownership of the film through the 1992 release of the Director's Cut and the 2007 Final Cut.

However, the theatrically released Director's Cut is *not* actually Ridley Scott's original vision for the film; rather it is a re-working that in the main pays lip service to the director's design for the film but actually comes out of commercial imperatives. Warners knew there was a market for a 'Scott' titled re-release because of the way 70mm copies of the work prints of the film were showing to full houses at film festivals in the US. Scott actually had little to do with the Director's Cut and the version that was released had continuity errors, and (violent) scenes that were in the original international release were missing. Nonetheless, in the Director's Cut the clumsy and patronising voice-over narration is all but removed, the city based ending is restored, along with the narrative ambiguity over Deckard's replicant status, and the 'unicorn reverie' is inserted in a dream sequence -- allowing this ambiguity to be foreshadowed earlier on in the film.

For Bukatman (1997) these changes, so resisted by Tandem Productions at the time of the original release, actually restore a visual and phonic level to the film effaced by the studio meddling. A restoration that bears out the vision of Scott the director:

> With the narration jettisoned, the film's formal opulence became more pronounced. As Deckard approaches police headquarters, the viewer is now free to contemplate the cityspace with him ... Freed of the teleology of a narration that told more than it should, the viewer could become more fully engaged by *Blade Runner*'s elaborate scenography.

Blade Runner: The Director's Cut was released in the US in September 1992 and on its opening weekend it made more money per screen than any other film on release. It continued to show to packed theatres a month later, and this success continued in Europe. This time critics also responded favourably, understanding second time around the complexity at the heart of its visually impressive dystopian vision. In one sense then, *Blade Runner* turned full-circle: from mainstream flop to cult classic it became, almost exactly ten years after its release, a mainstream commercial success. And over a decade further on, the success continues: recent years have seen a documentary of the production history of the film aired on American and British

TV; the production of this guide; an edited collection of new work revisiting the film edited by Will Brooker; and, of course, the 'Final Cut' in 2007, itself a precursor to a *five disc* DVD release. *Blade Runner* remains a cult classic that touches more people than Tandem Productions ever imagined it would.

5. Audiences

Films are, in the main, made for audiences to pay money to go and see. Audiences, through their choice of screenings and their response to films, can transform production trends and the decisions made about which films are made at the planning stage of film production. In one sense, audiences are sovereign. However, audiences are often measured by film companies only in terms of their potential size. A limited audience, or the likelihood of box-office failure for a mainstream, commercial film is to be resisted at all costs. Films are actually made to make money. Of course, mainstream films are made that do die at the box-office, and which only find a limited audience on their release.

The production and early distribution history of *Blade Runner* seem to bear this out: the classification struggles encountered during its production were driven by a fear that it wouldn't be a suitable vehicle for mainstream audiences; the test screenings confirmed this, and even with changes to the film's structure it did very poor box-office on its release. However, *what Blade Runner did next* confirmed the way audiences are more active, appreciative and diverse in their consumption of a film once the tag of mainstream flop has been removed by time, distance and context. Audiences are indeed sovereign and this is not purely connected to shaping production trends.

Instant Flop to Cult Classic

Although *Blade Runner* opened on 1,290 screens on its release, it took only $6.15 million on its opening weekend. Warners decided to pull *Blade Runner* from distribution weeks before the end of its intended run to air on their own Warner-Amex Satellite Entertainment Network. At this time there was a general widespread expansion of the cable television market and a massive growth in the home video market. This meant that *Blade Runner* was being 'released' into a burgeoning ancillary TV and video sector, desperate for product to fill its schedules and shelves. *Blade Runner* immediately found a cult audience on late night cable television, and in terms of video rental became a home box-office smash. Its reputation and importance grew; *Cityspeak* became the first fanzine dedicated to the film and at the 1983 World Science Fiction Convention it was voted the third most favourite science fiction film of all time. Dedicated websites, novels, fanzines, merchandising and conventions all followed until a *Blade Runner* universe emerged in and through the intertextual sites that one could go to explore and pay homage to the film.

So what has made *Blade Runner* such a cult science fiction favourite? The reasons are numerous. First, the film's visual detail and ambiguous plot demands repeat viewing. The film is, as Sammon (1999) suggests, 'an emotionally challenging, thematically complex work whose ideas and subtexts are just as startling as its justly famous production designs'. One has to return again and again to the film to get beneath the layering that Ridley Scott worked so hard to infuse the film with. The film is shot through with unanswered enigmas and dislocations that demand the attention of dedicated or not-so-dedicated fans. Of course, this produces slavish readings of its hidden meanings and trainspotter-like accounts of how these meanings can be read into the film. Websites, chatrooms, etc. provide a public space in which these accounts can be outed and tested. For example, *BladeZone – The Replicant Site –* offers users an interpretation of the meaning/rules of the chess game played by Tyrell and Sebastian in the film.

However, a polysemic or open ended and multi-layered text like *Blade Runner* also allows audiences to 'poach' their own new meanings from the film – and to offer new and extended narratives and versions that therefore keep the film in a cycle of perpetual renewal. *Blade Runner* is an open universe, with fans able to shape its meaning(s) to/for them in profound ways.

Second, in a related context, the visual excess and narrative complexity of *Blade Runner* seems to profoundly speak to people about the nature of their everyday lives. This language of crisis seems to go right to the heart of the matter of how fragmented the human condition is in the (post) modern world. It is as if, when people peer at the (under)belly of the future society depicted in *Blade Runner*, they see fragments of themselves looking back. The repulsion of *Blade Runner* is in part its attraction – one cannot help enter its world but one is frightened to do so because of what one will find of oneself there.

Third, the well-documented production history of the film contributes to giving the film a certain 'aura' or badge of artistic authenticity, an authenticity that one can argue is difficult to attach to other generic mainstream films. The troubles on the shoot, the enforced changes to the film after the test screenings, Scott's testimony of almost having to give blood to get the film made the way he wanted, and the heroic emergence of the Director's Cut adds to the sense of it being a unique artistic endeavour – and one in fact that nearly didn't make it at all to distribution. So, when one watches *Blade Runner*, especially the Director's Cut, one is watching a miraculous, awe-inspiring event not only textually but *extra-textually* as well. Cult fans want to belong to this unique cultural experience, and to share it with other like-minded devotees.

Finally, *Blade Runner* can be argued to be a transgressive film and transgression is often taken up by cult fans as an indicator of a film's true worth. *Blade Runner* transgresses the boundaries of genre, with its complex hybridity and wider media reference points. *Blade Runner* transgresses the norms of Classical Hollywood cinema with its gaps, emissions, and down-beat open ending. *Blade Runner* transgresses identity politics with its blurring of racial boundaries and human/cyborg dichotomies, and its implicit or implied critique of white identity formation. And *Blade Runner* transgresses politically with its sharp critique of corporate capitalism and consumption.

We live in a transgressive age: an age of new social movements and protest groups, and with it a corresponding decline in 'old' social formations such as class, family networks and national identity. We live in an age of greater sexual freedom and increased sexual and racial tolerance, but with this comes a giddy sense of boundary-less behaviour. We live in an age of the surveillance camera and the shopping mall, where privacy is difficult to find and the natural is buried beneath mounds of fashion branded goods and accessories. We live in an age of war and (on) terror, where rifle sight-lines and digitised bombings transform our image of things into a post-human mode of perception. We live in a transgressive age that is liberating and terrifying in equal measure. *Blade Runner* articulates, in a myriad of ways, what it is like to live in a transgressive age. As such, its cultural importance remains absolute.

6. Textual Analysis

The best way to get to understand how a film produces meaning is through close textual analysis. By breaking down a film into its main sequences or scenes, close textual analysis enables the critical reader to get beneath the skin of the film, to reveal its formal, narrative structure(s), its pleasures and its (sometimes hidden) ideological messages. Close textual analysis involves the assessment or deconstruction of shot, lighting, setting, performance, sound, editing, plot and narrative, both in terms of how they work in isolation and in terms of how they cohere to make a story meaningful.

An early scene from *Blade Runner* has been chosen for close textual analysis. The scene occurs at approximately 7 minutes into the film, and immediately follows Leon's cold-blooded shooting of Holden. In terms of classical narrative theory, therefore, we have just entered the disequilibrium stage of the film where a hero/ protagonist should now emerge.

Deckard Eats Noodles

Cityscape

The scene begins with a long, panoramic aerial shot of the futuristic metropolis. Densely packed skyscrapers dominate the frame as a police spinner moves towards the lens. A massive video advert of a Japanese geisha girl popping pills adorns one side of one skyscraper, filling the right of the frame with exotic flashes of colour and a degree of ambiguity since the advert has no product logo or English text to anchor down its meaning. Immediately the question emerges: what exactly are these pills for? But the answer is not directly given, and so just becomes one early example of the film's enigmatic narrative. This shot of the city is taken from within and directly over its quarters, and given that the first series of shots of the city which open the film were higher and further away, one is being given the impression of travel/ movement into the belly of this spatially dense environment. In fact, it is as if we are tracking the movement of the spinner(s) that appears in both shots, so that *this* spinner is itself given a degree of narrative motivation – as if it is transporting something important (*but what?*) into the heart of the city.

This shot of the city, of course, introduces the audience more fully to the technophobic : technophilia textures of the film, and its racial politics. In one sense the city appears foreboding and alienating: it is pitch black apart from the spinner, neon adverts and window lights that break through the cloak of darkness. In fact, the tightly packed skyscrapers seem to disappear into nothingness as if they go on forever *downwards*, into the metaphoric depths of hell. The oriental advertising hoarding is accompanied by Japanese sounding strings – sounds that are not concretely rooted in this shot but which seem to be rising up from *somewhere unseen and unknown below*. The sense that a creeping 'yellow peril' now populates and indoctrinates Los Angeles 2019 is being introduced to the audience. Of course, the notion of pill-popping and of omnipresent media persuasion (an advert for Pan-Am can also be found in the shot) draws attention to the centrality of artifice and surveillance to the film's narrative.

However, at the same time, there is also a degree of aesthetic beauty to the shot, not only in terms of film form/cinematography and the seamless use of special effects, but in the way technology on the screen is made to be gorgeous to look at. The spinner glows as it moves across the scene, the artificial lights appear like stars floating in a galaxy, and the red-lipped geisha girls are highly eroticised objects of beauty. In fact, the feel to the shot is arguably hypnotic.

Cityscape but looking upwards

The second shot in this scene is taken from below the cityscape, looking up at the skyscrapers that have so far only seen from above. The audience is now literally in the belly of the beast, viewing the city as if they are one of its inhabitants. The hard, physical horizontal and vertical lines of transport and communication that dissect the shot and the movement by blimps and spinners, across these axes, produce the sense that there is strict order in the city, a technological and rational order that doesn't seem to be touched by human hands. In fact, the city appears mechanically alive with grids and portals working in the same way as human arteries and veins. The sense that this isn't a place for (white) human kind is further emphasised by the electronically rendered voice coming from the blimp, offering (white) humans the promise of salvation but only in another world:

> 'A new life awaits you in the Off-world colony. The chance to begin again in a golden land of opportunity and adventure.'

The promise/slogan is reminiscent of the way Frontier America was sold to Europeans and as such narrates the demise or end of (European) spatial colonisation in Los Angeles 2019. America, so the sub-text begins to suggest, has now been re-colonised by the East and white Europeans, as a consequence, will have to colonise (move) elsewhere. The film makes this link to the past by having a horn-like sound reverberate around the shot, like an old Ocean Liner leaving the docks. However, one element effaced from this utopian representation of 'Off-world colony' life is the violent struggle that colonisation often involves. The film will later go onto suggest some of the horror of this through the exploits of the replicants, but at the moment given the claustrophobic and technological driven interior one is placed in, the Off-world seems to offer the potential of a better future, somewhere else, at least for white folk.

Pavement people

The third shot in this scene is a tracking crane shot that opens on a neon lit Chinese Dragon and then slowly moves down and into/through a hyper-busy shopping street, until it ends at eye-level on the as yet unnamed Deckard. In terms of the film's structure so far, this is the first time the audience have actually witnessed the inhabitants of this teeming metropolis going about their daily business. Until now the mechanical and the technological have dominated the view of the cityscape. The sudden rush and throng of people is, as a consequence, quite dislocating not least because the rigid lines of movement from the previous shot(s) seem to have been savagely broken. Chaos seems to reign in this scene with people moving anywhere they please, represented through nameless/faceless people getting in the way of the camera's movement through the street.

On the one hand, the city at this level appears futuristically dystopian; neon tipped umbrellas protect people from the incessant rain and the pollution which makes the streets murky – achieved through sparse, low-key lighting and the use of smog/smoke. Some of the people are masked and the sheer number of them suggests a population explosion. Not one tree or blade of grass grows in this scene. The 'yellow peril' is now given concrete representation, in large numbers, populating and owning the commerce (market stalls) of the shopping streets. On the other hand, the city at this level appears retrogressively dystopian – a dark city from the past. The dominant mode of transport for most of these people is foot, and the market traders selling noodles, etc. refer the audience to a 'Chinatown' that appears very like the one that existed *before* the film was made. Sentiments of film noir are also clearly present: the depressing rain, the low level light, the general down-beat mood; and the concrete and hard materials of the city feel like they have been appropriated from noir – they appear post Second World War rather than the stuff of some future apocalypse. To a degree, Deckard's introduction in this scene also echoes this retrogressive past.

As the camera moves through the street it is given a high degree of subjectivity: the camera seems to be looking for *someone or something* as it moves between the crowd. While Deckard is partly visible in the back of the frame, the murky and interrupted nature of the shot means that the audience cannot easily pick him out. His identity is in effect masked. In terms of the enigma code, therefore, tension and interest are being heightened by the ambiguity of whose subjectivity, if anyone, the camera is taking on, and of who (why) the camera is looking for? In terms of star studies, this delayed introduction to Harrison Ford also works in terms of audience pleasure: fans of Harrison Ford, who have come to see this film because of his presence in the film, are anticipating his arrival, they are waiting for the moment he *heroically* arrives on screen. Given Ford's star profile to date, as a high-adrenaline action hero in films such as *Star Wars*, audiences may be anticipating a spectacular arrival.

However, Ford's, or rather Deckard's, at first 'nameless' introduction in this scene is anything but heroic or spectacular. In fact, as the camera moves through the crowd Deckard seems to be deliberately hiding in the background, or at least is consciously keeping out of the way of the chaos of the crowd and the electronic eyes of the street, including the subjective (film) camera that is searching him out. When the camera arrives to capture him in long shot, he is leaning against the centre of a shop window that is ablaze with neon signs and filled with television screens. The dirty mac that he wears and the general dishevelled nature of his clothes suggest a vagrant like status. He is also located in a grim (ghetto area) part of town seemingly with nothing to do.

A man out of time

Deckard is reading a newspaper, eyes down. The connotations of this are complex. On the one hand, by reading a newspaper in a world of audio-visual signs Deckard is being revealed as a man out of time, out of place, clinging to the traditions of the past, not wanting to see things the way they really are. When the advertising blimp crosses overhead, again prophesising 'a new life awaits you' Off-world, Deckard looks on mournfully as if moving-off world would be a literal death for him.

On the other hand, because of the way/where he is standing he also seems to be 'plugged' into the neon signs and TV terminals that are situated behind him. Deckard, perhaps, is already being symbolically 'outed' or foreshadowed as a replicant, uneasy with the lie that he is a human. His mournful look to the blimp may be a sign that he doesn't belong here, on Earth, but should be 'Off-world' with the other replicants. The newspaper also marks him out as someone who is interested in finding things out, and so surveillance/investigation (of others if not himself) is going to be one of his personal attributes in the film. Generically speaking, then, science fiction begins to meld film noir with the police detective film. Hybridity is a fundamental constituent of this scene.

The scene continues with Deckard ordering noodles from a heavily stereotyped Chinese proprietor. Again, the camera takes up a subjective position so that Deckard appears to be being watched, but because of shot length and position, and abrupt cutting between shots, the subjectivity is given a more naturalistic or documentary feel here. This allows Deckard's melancholy to be given realist weight. He is probably a regular at the noodles bar he visits in the scene (he can use chopsticks with ease) and as such is being associated with the racially Other who populate the streets here. At this point in the film Deckard seems to be a resident of the lower levels, stuck in the belly of the beast. In terms, then, of both audience expectations of what Harrison Ford would/should be like in a film, and in terms of the 'arrival' of the classical heroic protagonist, *Blade Runner* undermines and undercuts the star/character performance model with real power.

The exchange that follows with the 'Chinaman' is interesting; Deckard orders in American English: the Chinaman at first appears not to understand and Deckard resigns himself to eating what is served up. They have failed or struggled to communicate with one another in a world where, the audience can only presume, English has been replaced as the dominant language. However, what immediately follows undercuts this reading.

'He says you are under arrest, Mr Deckard'

As Deckard begins to eat his noodles he is filmed at eye (low) level in relation to the sitting position he is in, and at medium distance. The faceless crowd continue to pass behind him, blurry figures in the back of the frame. Two figures approach Deckard but their faces/heads are out of the frame because of the camera angle and position employed. The audience cannot see them fully and so vision is again being interrupted. *Who are they and what do they want?* They address Deckard in a 'strange' tongue but he cannot understand them and so he asks, ironically it seems, the Chinaman to interpret. The Chinaman somehow miraculously masters the power of English and translates for him: 'He says you are under arrest, Mr Deckard'. The figure giving the arrest order is eventually revealed to be Gaff. However, very near the end of the film Gaff speaks to Deckard in English. So why the denial of being able to speak English in this scene? An answer is never given in the film but must link to the collapse of fixed and rooted identity positions – almost everyone in the film is involved in hiding or masking who they really are, to the point, it would seem, of losing the ability to communicate.

However, what this interchange does reveal is a great deal of narrative information about Deckard: he is a 'retired' Blade Runner, an ace ex-cop who can now be viewed not only on 'first impressions' as world weary and washed up, but as a killing machine beneath this worn out exterior (his initial introduction thus becomes *another type of enigmatic mask*, then). In short, the audience has been partially fooled by the 'look' of Deckard. He is to be the narrative anti-hero and the audience can expect him ('Harrison Ford') to take on the quest of hunting down the replicants with some skill. *Or then again, can they...?*

Deckard leaves peacefully with Gaff. The camera cuts to a long shot of a stationary police spinner – although the shot is crowded with other vehicles and the continued movement of people. Smoke, rain, noise and neon lights continue to fill the frame. One of the first signs that we see from the interior of the police spinner as it rises up off the ground is the word 'purge'. The violent connotations of this suggest that what is indeed being left behind, on the lower levels, should be purged, and given that Deckard is in the vehicle he seems implicated in the disgust. However, Deckard's presence in the vehicle complicates such assumptions, not least because if he is replicant he is also Other and belongs in the belly of this beast.

Spinner in cityscape

As the spinner takes off a series of interior and exterior shots are cut together so that Deckard and Gaff are observed flying the spinner, and the camera watches them observing the metropolis from aerial viewpoint. The higher the spinner flies the clearer, the more spectacular the scenery appears – vast edifices and structures compete with one another for domination of the frame and the electric glow of adverts, spinners, radiate the scene so that it *feels* warmer. Life appears better, less cluttered with people and poverty the higher one goes. The movement of the camera also changes: as it approaches an unnamed police headquarters the camera arcs and circles the building with balletic grace. Given the melodic, soft electronic tones of the vangelis soundtrack that accompanies the flight, the whole journey appears poetic. In fact, there are clear visual echoes here to the classical musical cued 'satellite' dance sequence in *2001*.

However, many of these impressions are undercut by the presence of Deckard, who has continued to eat his noodles in the cock-pit. Not only does this give him a laconic, take-it-as-it-comes attitude (*he has just been arrested* but doesn't seem to care), but also the noodles/eating works in terms of Deckard's identity crisis. By eating noodles from a street vendor, by bringing food into the glowing technophilia of the upper levels, he is confirming his human origins – he couldn't be further removed from the electronic dance on show. He belongs to the ghetto below even if he doesn't like it there. On the other hand, what is 'below' is also electronically encoded; this is where the escaped replicants have run to and where they feel safest. And so Deckard's relationship with the world below may actually be confirming his replicant status. To be sure, Deckard is a replicant ... *isn't he?*

Conclusion: What Does is Mean to be Human?

Perhaps the real story of *Blade Runner* is the story of what it means to be human in a world increasingly touched by technological invention and media intervention. The question the film seems to grapple with is: is *humanity* simply to do with *being human*, with mere corporeality – the material flesh and blood of people? Or is it value and behaviour driven so that replicants, made out of machines, can actually be more human, can act more humanely that the real humans in the film? As Tyrell himself says, 'more human *than* human'. The question is addressed in the film not only because technology can make human simulacra but also because the love of technology by humans, and the spread of media technology into all areas of social life, can make machines out of them. The irony of this is striking – the replicants will give anything to be human; Deckard is initially detached from his replicant status and appears more cold, calculating than when he later begins to question his human identity; Tyrell is all rational machine and seems incapable of true human emotion.

Of course, *Blade Runner* questions the nature of what it is to be human in even more complex ways because the machine : man dichotomy finds its way into the very fabric of the city, and the minutia of the plot and narrative.

Nonetheless, by the end of *Blade Runner* a degree of disintegration over these differences/questions seems to take place. Batty emerges as a converted religious figure: persecuted, looking for redemption, who decides to save his replicant nemesis from near certain death, rather than 'retire' him. Not only is he finally more human than Tyrell, his maker, he is ultimately more spiritual. Deckard, bruised, weak and confused is arguably outed as a replicant in the final few shots of the Director's Cut and as such has had his humanness (but not humanity) stripped away. He has very little time to live: very little time to enjoy the love he has just found with Rachael. Humanity cannot save him: even Batty cannot save him from this. Perhaps, then, the answer to the question, *what does it mean to be human?* is bound up with suffering, loss, alienation, existential confusion and with the unstoppable march of death. *Blade Runner* mediates on the postmodern nature of the human condition but ultimately the answers given are anything but comforting.

Postscript: The Final Cut 2007

The mythos of *Blade Runner* lives on. Since this guide was originally written in 2003 an excellent new edited collection on the franchise has been published (Brooker, 2005), and an immaculate, 'definitive' 2007 new version of the film theatrically released, along with three new DVD editions, including a 'Five-Disc Ultimate Collector's Edition' that includes four previous cuts, including the ultra-rare 'Workprint' Version.

Blade Runner: The Final Cut extends and complicates the central relationships in the film, and it adds further weight to the reading that Deckard is a replicant. The unicorn dream sequence has been extended, and its hypnotic but virtual quality re-signs it as a memory implant rather than a real human dream. It is a darker, more violent cut of the film. For example, Zhora's chase and death scene has been extended, as has her upsetting death rattle. Similarly, Batty's death scene, where a dove is released into a bright blue world, is now shot against a bleak, tumultuous-looking night sky.

Visually and aurally *Blade Runner* has been re-engineered using the most up-to-date improvements in film and audio technology so that is positively gleams in its technophilic rafters. A new digital print of the film was created from the original negatives, while the special effects were scanned in at 8,000 lines per frame, or four times the resolution used in most restoration film projects, so that they would appear sharper, deeper, *sensationally* textured. The soundtrack was also remastered, in 5.1 Dolby Digital surround sound, so that every rain drop, tower belch, and whisper resonates with splendor. The Final Cut, then, returns us to the dislocation that sits at the heart of the film: the future is ugly, heretical, and violent, with little hope for all who exist there; and yet it is also bejeweled and hypnotic, and simply gorgeous to screen-sense.

In these post-9/11 times, the film's own disintegration of the/any centre; of top/down; high/low; human/machine, seems perfectly apt for an age haunted by the imagined loss of safe, domestic space and of the borders of the self. The replicants become home-grown terrorists, created by the State, rising from the ashes of the exploitation of Late Capitalism to reek revenge on those who created them. Off-world is no longer an imagined utopia, but a ghastly inversion of Guantánomo Bay or Abu Ghraib. The film becomes a lesson on bio-power, or the attempt to take total control of the human body, to render it under complete control, to make it docile. *Blade Runner: The Final Cut* cuts deeply into the terror of the age.

Afterword (2016): *AfterHuman*

When *Blade Runner* was first released we were very much living in the analogue and (late) industrial age. Today, of course, the world is a digital one and for many people is fully augmented. In a very real sense the prophecies found in the future world of *Blade Runner* have become real and persistent. If the film has longevity it is not just because of its incredible sets, settings, finely drawn characters, and enigmas and mysteries, but because its imagination is one in sublime consort with the issues and fears that haunt the material present. So, what is it about the film that still today so (dis)enchants?

First, the film recognised that contemporary existence would be increasingly augmented, 'overlaid with dynamically changing information, multimedia in form and localized for each user' (Manovich, 2006: 220). It prophesised before the reality was fully born that we would exist in and through dynamic, information rich screens which would supply us with our everyday and everywhere needs. The fear today that augmentation will lead to us loving our screens more than we do each other is already found in the screenscapes of *Blade Runner*.

Second, *Blade Runner* recognised that the human condition was about to enter a fully post-human state, or the time of, 'Me++ …man-computer symbiosis' (Mitchell, 2003). This is the conceit of digital age science fiction film in general: not only does it replicate the core values, hopes and concerns of the post-human condition – prophesises on its future possibilities – but helps herald in the actual experience of humans living cybernetic lives. Science fiction film does this through its human-machine characterisations, cyborg narratives and spectacularly augmented world-building processes, such as is *Blade Runner*'s shimmering, commoditised LA 2019.

In *Blade Runner*, of course, we can't *quite* be sure who is human and who best articulates humanity. Very much of human conduct is tied to transnational commercial enterprises, which are involved in surveillance and control mechanisms and policing regimes. Deckard and Rachel are both versions of Paul Virilio's 'spastic', catastrophic urban figures that have found themselves bound up with the passive dreamscapes of new media technologies and interfaces; unable to exist freely in the world, they are controlled by the machine (1997: 20). That is, of course, until they resist the systems in place that seek to define and control them. Humanity, whether it is found in the human or post-human, cannot be snuffed out.

In contemporary life, the question of radical embodiment, and of the pleasures and contradictions of lived and living flesh, has become a dominant concern: one is increasingly asked to 'live themselves as code' (Hayles, 1993). N. Katherine Hayles (1999: 2) sees a present time in which 'coupling with intelligent machines' is so 'intense and multifaceted that it is no longer possible to distinguish meaningfully between the biological organism and the informational circuits in which the organism is enmeshed' (ibid.). The continuing appeal of *Blade Runner* speaks to the fusion experience since we are never entirely sure of Deckard's ontology (human or replicant) and so his love-making and (brute) intimacy with Rachel brings AI and human together.

There is another facet at play here: the rise of AI, machine intelligence, and how it will impact on social and political life. On the one hand, there is the fear that AI machines will replace humans and that in effect we are already a species on the verge of extinction. If one was to return to the lower levels of *Blade Runner* city one would see the flames of humankind being slowly extinguished as a super race emerges in the 'wings'. On the other hand, there is the hope that AI will free people from doing mundane jobs, opening up the possibility for a new leisure culture for all. The recent reports that AI robots will replace up to 40% of jobs in the new post-human economy either becomes a doomsday scenario or a new utopian dawn of freedom.

Fourth, *Blade Runner* in part builds its narrative out of the commercialisation of knowledge in the (coming) age of a computerised society where the grand narratives of pre-modernity no longer hold true. Everything is for sale in *Blade Runner* but the most precious commodity is knowledge – about one's origins, guilt, whereabouts and histories. Surveillance culture is writ large across the film.

In the contemporary digital age, truth and reason are seen to be held in the service of government, the military and big business (Lyotard, 1984). Knowledge and understanding is increasingly 'exteriorised', belonging with/to the corporate machine world. One is continually connected to this totalising machine but in a slave-to-master commodity-type relationship. All these tropes sit within and across the architecture of *Blade Runner*, making it a resistant and activist text, a critical dystopia that asks us to walk with the little people and to fight back against the machine. In the age of austerity politics and the post-GFC crisis, *Blade Runner* operates as a film that stands in the way of corporate greed.

Fifth, at the aesthetic level, *Blade Runner* prophesises on the way space and place was (is) being deterritorialised and reterritorialised, never simply grounded or rooted to a fixed location, but constantly remediated and reconstituted. In the contemporary science fiction film, space and place is always in flight and consequently one exists in a constant state of 'becoming nomad' (Mittag, 2009: 253). The expansive spatialisation of the digital image often draws attention to the unstable extremes of space and to the feeling that one is not very far away from the edge, from falling, flying or disappearing. As Kirsten Whissel argues,

> the new digital verticality is a technique for activating polarized extremes. Its abstract spatial coordinates are those of the zenith and the nadir, and its favourite location is the precipice, regardless of setting. (2006: 24)

Of course, *Blade Runner* gets to the precipice *before* the mechanics of digital special effects can puncture all axes before it. Deckard lives in the city without end, which cannot be easily navigated, and is only stopped from falling to his death by a fallen angel, who heralds from a planet off-world...

And why am I still interested in *Blade Runner*? I can see my youth, my fire, my dreams cast like a warm shadow over the film. It was my first true cinematic revelation (but viewed on a TV set at home) and it is where I saw visual poetry emerge and soundscapes swoon like Icarus in flight. And yet, it was its politics that also held me in its grip.

I was 15 when I first watched *Blade Runner*. Margaret Thatcher was in government in the UK, the attack on the working class and the trade union movement was well under way, and poverty in real terms was a daily occurrence for people in my neighbourhood. I knew and believed that things could only get better – that we didn't have to race towards our own utter negation. I lived with hope, in hope, with a passionate intensity. Today, I am not so sure: we have careered towards the apocalypse on so many fronts and in so many ways. *Blade Runner* has also become my yardstick for how bad things have got...

And yet, not entirely: If you, my refugee friend, homeless avatar, sick and frail parent, reach out your hand to mine, I will surely lift you up. *Blade Runner* is also hope.

SR 2016

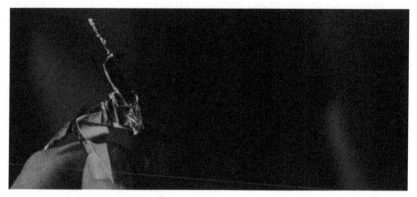

Augmented dreaming: Deckard holding origami unicorn

Bibliography and Filmography

Bordwell, David and Thompson, Kristin, *Film Art: An Introduction*, New York: McGraw-Hilll, 2002

Brooker, Will (ed.), *The Blade Runner Experience*, London: Wallflower, 2005

Bruno, Giuliana, 'Ramble City: Postmodernism and Blade Runner', in Kuhn, Annette (ed.), *Alien Zone*, London: Verso, 1990

Bukatman, Scott, *Blade Runner*, London: BFI Publishing, 1997

Desser, David, 'Race, Space and Class: The Politics of Cityscapes in Science-Fiction Films', in Kuhn, Annette (ed.), *Alien Zone II*, London: Verso, 1999

Dick, Philip K., *Do Androids Dream of Electric Sheep?*, New York: Doubleday Books, 1968

Dyer, Richard, *White*, London: Routledge, 1997

Grant, Barry Keith, '"Sensuous Elaboration": Reason and the Visible in the Science-Fiction Film', in Kuhn, Annette (ed.), *Alien Zone II*, London: Verso, 1999

Gunning, Tom, 'The Cinema of Attractions', in Elsaesser, Thomas (ed.), *Early Cinema*, London: BFI, 1990

Hayles, Katherine N., 'Virtual bodies and flickering signifiers', *October 66*, Fall 1993: 69-91

Hayles, Katherine, N., *How We Became Posthuman: Virtual Bodies in Cybernetics*, Chicago: University Of Chicago Press, 1999

Hoberman, J., 'Ten Years that Shook the World', *American Film* 10(8): 38–59, 1985

Kompare, Derek. "We Are So Screwed: Invasion TV", in *Flow*, Volume 3, Issue 6 (2005) http://jot.communication.utexas.edu/flow/?jot=view&id=1304 (accessed March 23rd 2006)

Kuhn, Annette (ed.), *Alien Zone*, London: Verso, 1990

Kuhn, Annette (ed.), *Alien Zone II*, London: Verso, 1999

Kuhn, Annette, 'Classical Hollywood Narrative', in Cook, Pam (ed.), *The Cinema Book*, London: BFI Publishing, 1999

Lyotard, Jean-François, *The Postmodern Condition*, Manchester: Manchester University Press, 1984

Manovich, Lev, 'The Poetics of Augmented Space', *Visual Communication* June 2006 vol. 5 no. 2 219-240

Mitchell, William J., *Me++ The Cyborg Self and the Networked City*, Cambridge MA: The MIT Press, 2003

Mittag, Martina (2009) 'Rethinking Deterritorialization: Utopian and Apocalyptic Space in Recent American Fiction', *Spatial Practices: An Interdisciplinary Series in Cultural History 2009*, Vol. 9, p251

Mulvey, Laura, *Visual and Other Pleasures*, Bloomington: Indiana University Press, 1989

Ono, Kent A., 'Domesticating Terrorism', in Harrison, Taylor and Projansky, Sarah (eds), *Enterprise Zones: Critical Positions on Star Trek*, Oxford: Westview Press, 1996

Ryan, Michael and Kellner, Douglas, 'Technophobia', in Kuhn, Annette (ed.), *Alien Zone*, London: Verso, 1990

Sammon, Paul M., *Future Noir: The Making of Blade Runner*, New York: HarperCollins, 1996

Sammon, Paul M., *Ridley Scott: The Making of His Movies*, London: Orion, 1999

Shay, Don, *Blade Runner: The Inside Story*, London: Titan Books, 2000

Sobchack, Vivian, 'Cities on the Edge of Time: The Urban Science-Fiction Film', in Kuhn, Annette (ed.), *Alien Zone II*, London: Verso, 1999

Stadler, Jane, 'Intersubjective, Embodied, Evaluative Perception: A Phenomenological Approach to the Ethics of Film', in *Quarterly Review of Film and Video*, 19(3): 237-248, 2002

Virilio, Paul, *Open Sky*. London: Verso, 1997

Wood, Robin, *Hollywood from Vietnam to Reagan*, New York: Columbia University Press, 1986

Magazines

Heavy Metal

Television

Documentary: *The Making of* Blade Runner (Barry Green II, 1997)

Documentary: *On the Edge of* Blade Runner (Andrew Abbott, 2000)

Filmography

Metropolis (Fritz Lang, 1927)

Double Indemnity (Billy Wilder, 1944)

Mildred Pierce (Michael Curtiz, 1945)

A Touch of Evil (Orson Welles, 1957)

Star Wars (George Lucas, 1977)

Alien (Ridley Scott, 1979)

E.T. The Extra Terristrial (Steven Spielberg, 1982)

Se7en (David Fincher, 1995)

Nil By Mouth (Gary Oldman, 1997)

Dark City (Alex Proyas, 1998)

War of the Worlds (Steven Spielberg, 2005)

Websites

BladeZone www.bladezone.com

Blade Runner – The Replicant Site www.blade-runner.com

CONSTELLATIONS
studies in science fiction film and TV

CLOSE ENCOUNTERS OF THE THIRD KIND

Jon Towlson

CONSTELLATIONS
studies in science fiction film and TV

INCEPTION

David Carter

Printed and bound by CPI Group (UK) Ltd, Croydon, CR0 4YY

13/04/2025

14656597-0001